I0471006

TruPlan: A Road Map to Financial Sanity

DEAN ROUSH

MARSUE ROUSH

DEDICATION

To all who struggle, which would be all of us.

CONTENTS

ACKNOWLEDGMENTS

Thank you to God Almighty, creator of all things, giver of life, author of salvation, and Father of our merciful savior Jesus Christ.

Part I - Principles of Personal Financial Management

"Take the first step in faith. You don't have to see the whole staircase, just take the first step." - Martin Luther King

This part contains detailed information that will help you learn to manage your personal finances effectively. The three chapters provide a step-by-step process that will prepare you financially for emergencies, put you in control of your spending, and enable you to eliminate your debt.

This page intentionally left blank

1 - Laying the Foundation

"A journey of a thousand miles must begin with a single step."

- Lau Tzu, Tao Te Ching

In this introductory chapter a road map is presented for the development of a successful financial plan and related support mechanisms. While there are many aspects to personal financial planning, the focus of this book will be the seven core milestones necessary to achieve financial stability. Let's jump right in and have a look at *TruPlan: A Road Map to Financial Sanity*.

TruPlan: A Road Map to Financial Sanity

1. Learn to live on a budget
2. Prepare for emergencies
3. Pay off your non-mortgage debt
4. Top off your emergency fund
5. Begin retirement fund contributions
6. Pay off your home mortgage early
7. Fund your retirement nest egg aggressively

1. Learn to live on a budget

This is such a simple thing to say but for many people it is very difficult to do. Living within a budget requires a change of how you think about money. Said another way, *"Spend less than you make"*. In Chapter Two you will learn how to prepare and follow a budget. A budget is a financial action plan. An action plan is defined as *"A series of actions, tasks or steps designed to achieve an objective or goal"*. The goal, of course, is to learn to manage your money well so that you are in control of your finances instead of your finances being in control of you.

2. Prepare for emergencies

Almost everyone has heard of Murphy's Law: *"Anything that can go wrong will go wrong"*. Hopefully Murphy will not show up very often, but everyone can remember times of unexpected expenses for car repairs, medical bills, etc. A budget is a plan for the expected expenses, not the unexpected ones.

Be ready for the unexpected by taking the following steps:

- Establish an initial emergency fund of at least $500.
- Execute an inexpensive, simple will and medical power of attorney for each adult member of your household.
- Purchase term life insurance for each adult member of your household.
- Acquire medical insurance coverage for all household members.

Do not misuse the emergency fund. The money should only be used for true emergencies: unplanned car repairs, unplanned doctor visits, etc. Refer to *Chapter 5 - Insurance* in Part II for more information on the types and amounts of insurance coverage you need. Also refer to *Appendix F – Online Resources* for information that can help you to obtain legal wills and medical powers of attorney at low cost.

3. Pay off your non-mortgage debt

In today's world it is very common for people to owe money. The Bible teaches us that the *"borrower is servant to the lender"* (Proverbs 22:7). This verse simply means that as long as you owe money, then you are not in control of your finances. Refer to *Chapter 3 - Debt Elimination* for a more complete discussion of this topic.

4. Top off your emergency fund

Once you have paid off all of your non-mortgage debt, it is time to more fully insulate yourself against the ups and downs of life that can bring crippling financial hardship. The loss of a primary income due to death, economic downturn, sudden health problems, divorce, or other reasons is not uncommon. Fully load your emergency fund (equal to six months of expenses) in a money-market account at a local community financial institution.

5. Begin retirement fund contributions

Modify your budget to put money aside for retirement. Your age and income may affect how much you budget, but in general your goal should be fifteen percent of your gross income. If you work for an employer that provides a company match for a 401K (or similar) plan, contribute at least enough to take full advantage of the company match.

If you do not have a 401K or similar plan through your employer then set up a Regular IRA or Roth IRA account through a reputable brokerage firm or your local financial institution. Your retirement contribution should be at least fifteen percent of your salary. Refer to *Chapter 7 - Investing* in Part II for more information.

6. Pay off your home mortgage early

It is possible and highly desirable to own a home without an accompanying mortgage loan. This is especially important at retirement. By paying off your mortgage early, you will free up extra dollars to help build your retirement nest egg. This is especially important if you start working on your retirement fund later in life.

There are a couple of ways to accomplish this goal. One way is to send in extra payments to be applied to the principal of your existing mortgage. The second way is to refinance your home for less time than the remaining term on your existing loan and/or for a lower effective interest rate. Refer to *Chapter 4 - Housing* in Part II for a more complete discussion of this topic.

7. Fund your retirement nest egg aggressively

Retirement is on the horizon and approaching quickly! The TV, car, and house are paid for, free and clear. The most important thing you can do now is shore up that retirement account as quickly as possible. Reconfigure your budget one more time and squeeze every last penny into that 401K, Regular or Roth IRA or other retirement account.

This is when a retirement planning specialist can give you some insight into just how beneficial extra contributions can be to your retirement nest egg. Refer to *Chapter 7 - Investing* in Part II for a more complete discussion of this topic.

Support Team

As the planning process begins, think about recruiting a support team. A good support team consists of wise counselors and accountability partners. Consider the following Bible verses:

"let the wise listen and add to their learning, and let the discerning get guidance--" - *Proverbs 1:5*

"For lack of guidance a nation falls, but many advisers make victory sure."- Proverbs 11:14

What do counselors and accountability partners do? A counselor will help you analyze a situation and make a decision or create a plan appropriate to the circumstances. An accountability partner will know what your plan is and encourage you on an ongoing basis to keep making the necessary sacrifices to stay on that plan.

Having wise counselors and accountability partners can really make a difference in your ability to succeed. Try to find two or three friends, pastors, or other mature individuals that are well-grounded in Biblical-based money management practices that are willing to serve in either or both of these roles. Mature counselors should be able to be honest with you ("tough love") when you are headed down the wrong path. These individuals should be invited to join your support team only after receiving a good recommendation from someone you personally know and whose judgment you trust.

What is the right number of counselors? Having only one robs you of the ability to 'cross-check' the advice you receive. On the other hand, if you have too many you will become frustrated when they disagree on particular issues. Disagreement is a good thing, because it can spur healthy debate. Too much disagreement brings only confusion. Two or three counselors should be sufficient. Listen to your chosen counselors carefully. Compare what each has to say about how you should handle a given situation.

Whenever possible, select team members that are not family members. Family members giving financial advice may feel insulted if the advice is discounted or ignored. It is better to maintain those relationships and seek wise counsel elsewhere.

In some situations it may be advisable to seek professional (paid) advice. The selection process for a professional counselor should be the same as it is for a personal counselor. However, the advice given by a professional does not necessarily trump the opinions of other members of your support team. There should always be a significant measure of harmony of the recommendations received. If the harmony is absent, then additional prayer and counseling should be sought before proceeding with a new plan. Remember that God's timing is not our timing and it may be best to wait until a clear picture for action emerges and peace is present.

And finally, do not fail to pray regularly to our Father in Heaven and ask Him to grant wisdom, direction and clarity to both you and to your counselors.

"Do not be anxious about anything, but in everything, by prayer and petition, with thanksgiving, present your requests to God. 7 And the peace of God, which transcends all understanding, will guard your hearts and your minds in Christ Jesus."- Philippians 4:6-7

Organization

As with any endeavor, it is always very helpful to be organized. There are many organizational styles, but the important thing is to have a system that works for you. All of your financial information should be kept neatly in a secure location. This includes pay, medical, bank, credit-card, pension and other financial or sensitive records.

Financial records should be stored in a locked area to keep visitors and family members (other than spouse) from accessing them. Use a locking fire-proof file cabinet if possible. Computerized records should be protected using a strong password (consisting of a combination of eight or more upper- and lower-case letters, numbers and special characters). Never share your password (except with your spouse) or leave it written down in a place where it could be found by others.

This page intentionally left blank

2 - Your Financial Action Plan

"If you fail to plan, you plan to fail." – Unknown

Completing *TruPlan: A Road Map to Financial Sanity* in the prescribed order will help to put you on solid financial ground when dealing with life's issues. The implementation of these steps begins with the preparation of your financial action plan. Proverbs 21:5 says *"The plans of the diligent lead to profit as surely as haste leads to poverty."*

In the previous chapter a budget was characterized as a 'financial action plan'. There are two equally important aspects to your budget: Design and Execution. In this chapter you will learn how to accomplish both of these tasks successfully.

Design

The process of designing a proper financial action plan (budget) entails three steps:

1. List all income sources and amounts.
2. List all expenses.
3. Realistically adjust either or both until income exceeds expense.

Budgets are typically created and managed on a monthly basis, because a calendar month coincides with the normal cycle for paying bills in modern society. A new written budget should be prepared before each month begins. If budgeting is new and unfamiliar to you, ask your wise counselors for assistance.

A template (form) is presented in *Appendix B – Budget Template* that you can use to create your budget each month. The template is somewhat lengthy but is designed to serve as a checklist to make sure you remember everything. The standard descriptions in the template can be changed to enter items that are specific to your financial situation. Now is a good time to look it over.

Each item of income and expense for the month should be listed on the budget form. Total income should always equal or exceed total expense. If not, then review both the income and expense items and determine where adjustments can be made. Be sure to include expenses that are due annually or semi-annually (or at other irregular intervals), such as car insurance or life insurance payments.

Be realistic! Do not overstate your income for the month. Do not include overtime pay or bonuses unless you are sure it will be paid. Do not omit expenses that you know will occur during the month just to make the budget balance. And no, a night out on the town on Friday night is not an essential! No cheating! Use a computer spreadsheet or calculator and add everything up twice to verify your figures.

For couples, all income and all expenses should be included for both spouses. In a marital environment there should be no 'yours' or 'mine'. You are a team and both spouses are equal partners (Genesis 2:24). Again, include commissions, overtime, bonuses, etc in your income only if there is a very great likelihood the amounts will be paid to you during the budget period. If your income is irregular, you must set aside extra income received during peak earning times to be available to pay household expenses during lean times. Include all expenses that must be paid during the budget period.

Execution

The execution of your written budget is where the rubber meets the road! You must spend money only in accordance with your budget plan for the month. Do not charge something on a credit card (you cut those in half already, right?) to defer paying for an expense until the following month. If you have a problem with writing too many checks (or if you cannot properly manage a checking account or do not have a checking account) then consider using an envelope system. Refer to *Appendix H – Checkbook Management* for more information on maintaining a checkbook.

With an envelope system just put the money for each budgeted expense into a separate envelope with the name of that expense marked on the front. For additional convenience, you could write the amount (if known in advance) and due date of each bill on the envelope. If you are paid more often than once a month then some envelopes will be filled from the first pay check, some from the second, etc. Never leave envelopes containing money in an unsecure location!

Do not use the money in each envelope for any purpose other than the named expense. For example, if you budget $300 for food for the month, take that envelope (or some of the money in it) with you when you go to the grocery store. Pay for your groceries from the money in that envelope.

Make sure you buy some non-perishable groceries for times when you are out of money (dry beans, etc). This way when the money is gone you will still be able to eat! Learn to use restraint so that the money is not spent too early in the month.

If you stick to the plan and do not spend money on un-budgeted items, then you are on track! Congratulations! If you have an unexpected expense (Murphy shows up) and have to dip into your emergency fund, well, guess what…you will still succeed because you had a plan for that too!

Even though you make a mistake or two along the way do not become discouraged and stop trying. Many people learning to live on a realistic budget have succeeded and you can too! Budget planning and execution is a straightforward process. The hard part is your willingness to change your old habits. You may have a properly designed budget but find yourself struggling to control your spending. Do not forget your accountability partners! They will offer important encouragement to help you resist the urge to overspend.

Progress Measurement

Success in personal finance requires planning, commitment, hard work and time. But how can success be recognized? There is an easy way to measure how much progress is being made. The process involves periodically (perhaps quarterly) taking a 'snapshot' of your financial situation and comparing that snapshot with previous ones.

The snapshot is a simple list and total of everything you own (assets) and everything you owe (liabilities). The difference between what is owned and what is owed is called net worth. If net worth increases over time then success is being achieved. If net worth decreases over time then the plan is not working and adjustments should be made.

The snapshot is formally known as a 'Statement of Financial Position', or less formally called a 'balance sheet' or 'financial statement'. Refer to *Appendix A – Financial Statement Template* for an example.

This page intentionally left blank

3 - Debt Elimination

"Keep skunks and bankers at a safe distance." – *Old Farmer's Advice*

There is no better way to begin a discussion on debt than by quoting from Proverbs 22:7: *"The rich rule over the poor, and the borrower is servant to the lender."* Most Americans believe that slavery was abolished when President Abraham Lincoln delivered his famous *'Emancipation Proclamation'* speech in 1863. However, by observing typical lifestyles in America today, it seems that slavery is still rampant! Slavery due to indebtedness is almost universal. To be truly free you must get out of debt and stay out of debt!

Getting Into Debt

There are many ways to incur debt, but all debts will fall into one of two broad categories: Secured, and Unsecured. Debt is 'secured' when collateral is taken by the lender (i.e. car title). Collateral pledged to secure a loan can and will be repossessed by the lender if the borrower refuses to pay or is unable to pay back the loan. Debt is 'unsecured' if no collateral is taken. Either way, debt represents a moral (Ecclesiastes 5:5) as well as legal obligation to repay. Table 3-1 presents examples of different types of debt and the category to which they belong:

Table 3-1   Examples of secured and unsecured debt

Secured Debt	Unsecured Debt
Mortgage loan	Credit card\revolving charge
Home equity loan	Signature\payday loan
Reverse mortgage	Tax refund loan
Vacation time-share	Student loan
Vehicle loan	Medical debt
Rent-To-Own contract	Unpaid tickets\fines\legal fees
Pawn ticket	Co signed loan\guaranteed

Take special note of the last item on the right-hand list. When you co-sign or guarantee a loan for someone else, you have incurred an obligation and taken on personal risk/responsibility. Co-signed or guaranteed loans may be unsecured or secured, depending on a lender's requirements. The risk to the co-signer or guarantor is viewed by the lender almost as if you borrowed the money yourself (Proverbs 11:15). Likewise, if you agree to pledge any of your assets (such as a bank certificate of deposit) to secure another person's loan, you have incurred personal risk at least to the extent of the value of the assets pledged, and possibly more if the debt is not repaid by the borrower.

You must work to rid yourself of all of these risky obligations. Never guarantee, co-sign, or pledge collateral to loans for anyone (especially family and friends). Allow professional lenders to provide those loans. If the borrowers are turned down by professional lenders, it is because they are not willing to take the risk. Neither should you. RED FLAG! Think about it! If you want to help someone, give them a cash gift or other help that is reasonable according to your own financial situation and only under the assumption that you never expect to be repaid.

An old German proverb says *"Money lent to a friend must be recovered from an enemy."* An old American proverb says *"Before borrowing money from a friend decide which you need most."* For further study and discussion of this issue read: Acts 20:35, I Timothy 6:8, Psalms 37:21, Proverbs 17:18, Matthew 7:6, and II Thessalonians 3:10.

Many people make the case that borrowing money is a great way to increase your credit-worthiness. In modern society, a person's credit worthiness is most often measured on a scale known as the FICO Score©. By having a higher FICO Score, a person has a greater ability to borrow money. This greater ability to borrow encourages more borrowing. Your goal is having no debt and consequently a FICO Score doesn't matter. Gaining financial freedom is not about having a great credit score; it is about not needing a credit score at all!

The Cost of Debt

Regardless of the types of debt you have, most debt incurs interest. Lenders make money by charging interest and fees on the money they have out on loan. You may be able to obtain a truly interest-free loan from family members, special-interest groups, or the government. Other organizations offer interest-free loans that are not actually interest-free, but have hidden fees or use other gimmicks to profit from those loans.

Financial institutions loan money to make money. Their goal is not to 'help' you. They borrow money at a low rate of interest from depositors and turn around and loan that money back to borrowers at a higher rate of interest. The difference in the two rates of interest is commonly called the 'spread'. You should refer to it more appropriately as the 'penalty'. Every time you finance a car, vacation, or television you are penalizing yourself with the significant extra costs of borrowing. You can and should avoid those penalties by saving up and paying cash for those cars, vacations, and televisions.

Setting aside the concept that borrowing money is expensive and a bad idea, loans can also have costs that are not purely financial. Stress, loss of choice, too much focus on materialism, and strain on personal relationships can all be associated with the struggle to repay debt. It is an often-cited fact that disputes over money is one of the leading causes of divorce in America today.

As mentioned in the previous section, it is never a good idea to lend money to a family member, friend, or co-worker. It is also never a good idea to borrow money from these individuals (or from anyone). It changes the dynamics of your relationship with them and if you struggle to repay the debt your relationship could be forever damaged.

Debt Collection

If you are having trouble paying the bills and fall behind, you may begin receiving calls from bill collectors or debt collection agencies. There are federal laws that protect consumers by governing the behavior of debt collectors. *Appendix L – Summary of Your Rights under the Fair Debt Collection Practices Act* contains a summary of your rights related to debt collection. Also, *Appendix K – Summary of Your Rights Under the Fair Credit Reporting Act* provides a summary of federal laws that protect consumers as it relates to anyone that reports your credit history to credit reporting agencies, employers or others.

Always keep records of your loan contracts, payments, and any correspondence or communication with lenders. Make notes of conversations with lenders. Always means "always" because you must, for *the rest of your life* (what did we say about freedom?), be prepared to prove that you have fulfilled all of your financial obligations. There is a statute of limitations on how long debt collectors can use the court system to force you to pay. The limits vary by state law and type of debt, but generally run three to fifteen years. Debt can remain on your credit reports for as long as seven years even if the statute of limitations has expired.

Proof of payment can only come from the documents provided to you by those lenders that indicate your loans have been fully satisfied. Always ask for, and keep, written statements showing that your debts were "Paid in Full"! If you pay any amounts in cash (not recommended) always obtain and keep a receipt until you have final written proof that your debt is paid in full.

If you fall behind in your payments, do not give collectors electronic access to your checking, credit card, or other account. Many collectors do not live up to verbal agreements and will take more money from the accounts than you agreed to give. If you have already given electronic access, then close your account and move it to another financial institution. This recommendation is not made to help you avoid paying your obligation but to allow you maintain control over your money and your budget.

If a lender or collector offers to settle a debt for less than the amount owed, always get the offer in writing before making any such settlement payments. Read all loan documents or settlement offers carefully so that you will fully understand the terms of the agreement. Ask your wise counselors to review any agreements before you act on them.

Refinancing Debt

There are very few situations where it makes sense to refinance an existing debt. In general, you should dismiss the notion of getting a debt consolidation loan or home equity loan. Also, never borrow from your retirement plan to pay off other debt (or for any reason). In spite of your best efforts you cannot borrow your way out of debt.

Mortgage debt can and should be re-evaluated periodically. If you have an adjustable-rate mortgage (ARM), balloon, or interest-only mortgage loan then you should, in most cases, attempt to convert that loan to a fixed-rate mortgage. By definition, ARM interest rates can rise and dramatically increase your house payment. As evidenced by the real estate bust of 2007-2011, many families have been forced into foreclosure due to ARM interest rate adjustments. If you plan to sell the house or pay off the mortgage in the immediate future, then refinancing is not recommended.

Bankruptcy

Bankruptcy is a legal status conferred to an individual or organization by a court order when that individual or organization is deemed unable to pay debts owed to creditors. Certain types of debt including child support and alimony, student loans, back taxes, and restitution for criminal acts cannot be eliminated. A bankruptcy filing will remain on a credit report for ten years. Bankruptcy is a broad topic that is beyond the scope of this book. Bankruptcy is not a recommended option in most cases.

Getting Out Of Debt

When you get serious about eliminating your debt there are a couple of things you can do to get started on the right foot. Cut up all of your credit cards and stop borrowing money. Right now! Will Rogers once said *"If you find yourself in a hole, the first thing to do is stop digging."* In this case, stop charging!

To begin the process of getting out of debt, you must know exactly where you are starting from. Request a copy of your credit report from one of the national credit-reporting agencies. Review the report and look for open credit obligations. Refer to *Appendix F – Online Resources* for links that will provide more information on how to obtain and understand what is in your credit report. Be sure to use the link provided in the appendix to avoid the many sites that look 'official' but attempt to charge unnecessary fees!

Avoid doing business with debt-relief services. These services often charge up-front fees and usually provide little or no improvement in your debt level. The claims for debt-reduction are usually significantly overblown.

Look for ways to work directly with creditors to pay off or reduce debt. Many creditors are willing to reduce the balance of a debt if it increases the probability that they will get paid. However, never settle a debt with a creditor unless you are given the terms of settlement in writing. Discuss your negotiating plan with your wise counsel and ask them to review the written settlement offer before you send money to pay off the debt. Remember, never give a creditor electronic access to your bank account or credit card (send a money order instead).

Find ways to increase your income, such as taking a part time job. Use the extra income to pay down debt faster. If you have vehicle payments, sell one or more vehicles and/or trade down to a cheaper vehicle with little or no loan payment. If you owe more on a mortgage or vehicle loan than the house or vehicle is worth, try working with your lender on a short sale.

In a short sale the seller must make up the shortage in cash or, more likely, by taking out a loan for the difference between the sales price and the loan payoff amount. Taking a loan for the difference may be acceptable if it helps reduce the overall indebtedness of the borrower and if the borrower does not have enough cash on hand to pay the shortfall. Executing a short sale is usually a better option than a foreclosure or repossession if it can be worked out among the parties.

While keeping your initial emergency fund intact, pay down as much debt as possible with any and all extra cash you have. Reduce your lifestyle. Every dollar that you do not spend on lifestyle is a dollar that can be applied to outstanding debt. Refer to *Appendix G – Money Saving Tips* for specific ideas on how to spend less money.

You must stop subsidizing the lifestyles of others while you still have debt. This includes supporting people that live in your home that are capable of being self-supporting. This also includes people that do not live in your home but that you support financially in some way (adult children, friends). You cannot afford to help others in any significant way until you yourself are on sound financial footing (debt free). That time will come later.

While there are many strategies available to eliminate debt, the 'debt snowball' method is recommended. In a nutshell, the debt snowball strategy is to list all your debts in order from smallest balance to largest balance and pay off the debt with the smallest balance first. Apply all available extra cash within your balanced budget each month to the smallest balance. For all other debts pay the minimum required payment amount only. Move on to the next smallest balance when the smallest balance is paid off. Repeat the process until all of your debt (except your mortgage) is paid.

The snowball method provides you with a psychological advantage. You can actually see progress occurring as each debt is eliminated. Would you prefer to see one of your payments eliminated after three months of effort or after thirty months of effort?

Undoubtedly, every situation is a little different. As previously mentioned, you are encouraged to engage your wise counselors for support as you work through your debt elimination plan (Proverbs 16:9). If you have good counsel and can stick to a realistic budget then you will not need the services of credit counseling or debt consolidation agencies. These agencies do for you (for an extra fee) what you can do yourself.

Starting now, pay cash for everything! If you don't have the cash you can't afford it!

Part II – Significant Financial Topics

"Opportunity is missed by most people because it is dressed in overalls and looks like work." - Thomas A. Edison

When you have achieved an understanding of how to control spending through the budget management process you are ready to move on to more advanced topics in personal finance. This part includes chapters that explain important financial concepts related to housing, insurance, transportation, and investing.

The information contained in the following chapters is presented at a very high level and is not intended to be a complete discussion of the topics. It is intended to help you become aware of the important issues these types of transactions involve. Because transactions related to these topics usually involve significant financial risk, it cannot be emphasized enough that you should consult your wise counselors when considering taking action.

This page intentionally left blank

4 - Housing

"Good advice is like good paint - it only works if applied." – Unknown

This chapter deals with the relative merits of renting vs. buying a home. At the outset, it is not advisable to take on a home mortgage while you still have other debt. Home ownership can be a great investment at the right time in your life, but not while you are working to become debt free.

As a general rule, your payment for basic housing (rent or mortgage payment) should be no more than twenty-five percent of your monthly net income. Utility costs are not to be included in this calculation. For mortgage payments, the amount should also include the escrow portion set aside for taxes and insurance. Your realtor or mortgage lender can help you accurately estimate how much your mortgage and escrow payment amounts will be. Refer to *Appendix F – Online Resources* for links to loan calculators to help with these estimates.

Consider the full cost of housing when deciding whether to rent or own (Luke 14:28-30). Ask the seller or landlord to provide a listing of the actual utility costs for the most recent twelve months. Do your research before entering into a binding contract so there will be no surprises later when it is too late to back out!

Renting\Leasing

Renting (or leasing) is always the best choice while you are paying off existing debt. Renting a home also gives you an opportunity to experience living in a particular neighborhood before committing to buy a house there. While some landlords will agree to an initial month-to-month arrangement, it is common to sign a lease that requires a six- or twelve-month commitment (followed by a month-to-month arrangement). Be sure to read the terms of the agreement carefully before signing. Check for terms relating to damage and pet deposits, advance payments, maintenance, etc. It is always beneficial to have your wise counselors review the agreement with you before signing.

Lease\Purchase Agreements

If you are considering an opportunity to lease-purchase a home, you should have the contract reviewed by competent legal counsel, a licensed realtor, and your wise counselors before you sign on. At a minimum, you should be able to withdraw from the purchase part of the contract without penalty at any time before committing to actually purchase the home.

In addition, you should not be obligated to (and should not) make any additional payments toward the purchase amount, or make costly improvements to the property, in anticipation of purchasing the home. Wait until you have met all of the recommendations listed below before committing to purchase a home, whether the agreement is a lease-purchase arrangement or otherwise.

Home Ownership

A home is usually the most expensive purchase you will ever make. It is also potentially one of the most emotionally and financially rewarding choices you will ever make. Making a house into a home that is decorated with your personal style is truly a labor of love and a great source of pride and satisfaction. As they say *"A man's home is his castle"*!

Purchasing a home usually results in new debt. While it is acceptable to have a mortgage under the right conditions it is not acceptable to pile new debt on top of existing debt. There are usually significant closing costs associated with buying a home. Additionally, most new homeowners will want and/or need to spend extra money at move-in time to spruce up the house with new draperies, accent rugs, carpet and paint, landscaping, and other frou-frou that makes a house a home. Do not forget to take these expenses into account when planning your home purchase. Refer to *Appendix F – Online Resources* for links to rent-vs.-buy calculators.

Good stewardship implies that you will adequately maintain the home to protect your investment (Proverbs 27:23). When the plumbing breaks or a new roof is needed you cannot simply call the landlord. You must be able to pay cash for those repairs. You should understand, and prepare for, all of the risks and rewards before committing to such a significant obligation. Be sure to have appropriate inspections performed beforehand by competent licensed inspectors. Obtain heating/cooling, plumbing, foundation and roofing inspections at a minimum. Depending on geographic location additional inspections may be appropriate (i.e. mold, termites). Your realtor can help you locate competent inspectors.

Never purchase pre-manufactured housing (mobile homes). While appearing to be attractive and more affordable, pre-manufactured housing depreciates like an automobile instead of appreciating in value like traditional housing.

Do not purchase the largest house on the block. You will have trouble getting your money out of it when it comes time to sell. And yes, at some point in the future you (or your heirs or lenders) will sell that house.

Consider the location where you are thinking of buying a house. Does it matter what school district you want to live in? How high are the property taxes and other assessments in this neighborhood? How far away are workplaces and schools for your family? What public transportation options are available? Is the home you are considering located on a too-busy or too-noisy street? Is it hard to find? Is it located in a flood or hurricane zone? Has the home been adequately maintained?

A competent, licensed independent realtor (along with your other wise counselors) will provide much needed guidance to help you make the best home buying (or selling) decision for your situation. Realtors can perform a formal market analysis, look at actual recent sales transactions of comparable homes and help you determine a fair market value for the home you are selling or thinking of buying. Realtors also provide the benefit of their professional experience when it comes time to prepare, review, and negotiate contracts for the sale or purchase of a home. Ask your wise counselors to help you select the right realtor.

Home Buying Guidelines

Buy a home only if ALL of the following conditions are true:

- You have no other debt (including existing mortgages).
- The payment (principle, interest, taxes, and insurance) will be no more than 25 percent of your monthly net income.
- You will have a fixed-rate mortgage with a term of fifteen years or less.
- You pay at least five percent of the purchase price plus your closing costs in cash.
- You have adequately prepared for emergencies (TruPlan Step Four).

- You will not be a co-owner of the home with anyone other than your spouse.
- You plan to live in the home for at least three years.
- Your employment picture is stable now and into the foreseeable future.
- You are in a stable relationship if married or planning to marry.
- You are represented by a competent licensed independent realtor.
- The home has been given a good report by one or more competent licensed inspectors.
- The title to the home will be insured by a title policy issued by a reputable, financially stable vendor.

Home Repair and Remodeling

Home ownership has many advantages. But it also has disadvantages. It is extremely important to protect a large investment such as a home by keeping it in good order. When something breaks it should be fixed promptly and properly. Many home owners can make many repairs themselves, but sometimes it becomes necessary to bring in a qualified contractor with the right experience and tools.

In addition to keeping a home in tip-top shape, home owners occasionally want to expand or remodel their home. The cost to remodel should be carefully calculated. Choosing how to pay for remodeling is also an important decision. A good rule of thumb is to skip the remodel if the adjusted market value of the home after remodeling will exceed the average market value of other comparably-sized homes in the same neighborhood. Also, do not remodel a house to the extent that it becomes more than what the existing neighborhood reflects in style and amenities.

Regardless of the type of work to be done around the house, the selection of a qualified and honest contractor is an important part of the process. Take plenty of time to choose a reputable, experienced contractor to handle your project.

Here are some guidelines for selecting a contractor:

- Get multiple written detailed estimates, even for small jobs, to compare costs and plans.
- Written estimates should specify the time frame for completion.

- Search for consumer reviews and complaints for contractors of interest.
- Check contractor-supplied references from several previous customers.
- Verify that contractors insurance coverage exists and is sufficient.
- Check with licensing boards to make sure contractors are appropriately licensed.
- Verify business permits issued by your city to potential contractors.
- Get the estimate and maximum hourly rate in writing in case the job wraps up quickly.
- The contractor should not ask for a down payment that would exceed ten percent of the total contract value.
- Final payment (at least ten percent) should occur only after <u>all</u> work is inspected and finished to your satisfaction.
- If a lien was filed by the contractor, make sure it is released when final payment is made.

This page intentionally left blank

5 - Insurance

"Anything that can go wrong will go wrong" - Murphy's Law

As you begin the journey to financial sanity it is time to really insulate yourself financially against some of the major problems that can happen in life. Death, serious illness, natural disasters, accidents and other events can bring crippling financial hardship. Hedging against such problems is called risk management.

One definition of an accident is *"a mishap or unforeseen and unplanned event or circumstance, often with lack of intention or necessity"*. It implies a generally negative outcome. If you are immune to accidents then skip this chapter. In fact, close this book and go on with your life. Otherwise, keep reading because the information presented in this chapter is all about good stewardship.

Risk management is not about preventing events that bring about financial hardship. It is about sharing (reducing) the financial burden that often comes when a hardship occurs. A common form of risk management is buying insurance. Insurance is your financial back-up plan if and when disaster strikes. Insurance companies have the financial resources to absorb the high costs associated with those hardships.

There are many forms of business and personal insurance. The focus in this chapter is on personal insurance for life, health, property and other coverage. Individuals buy such insurance to offset all or a portion of the specified costs if and when an insurable event occurs. Insurance coverage plays a significant role in *Step 2 – Prepare for Emergencies* in the TruPlan Road Map.

Good stewards realize that growing a family and building wealth is a tremendous blessing. Protecting your family and assets is what good stewardship is all about. Luke 14:28-30 talks about counting the cost before beginning an endeavor. The cost of insurance should always be included.

Remember that insurance is a product. Many vendors are eager to sell insurance coverage. Do not just buy from the lowest bidder. As with any product or service, be sure to shop for the best value and verify the integrity, financial stability, reputation, and customer service ratings of the vendor.

Life Insurance

The purpose of life insurance is to provide financial protection for your family if you were to die unexpectedly (it happens!) If you are the primary breadwinner, your income will disappear but your spouse and children will still have unmet needs. If you are the primary caretaker for your children then your spouse will need assistance with raising the children when you are gone. Either way, the life insurance policy death benefit amounts should be at least five times the lost annual incomes of the primary parties in the household, perhaps double that amount if young children are involved or if one spouse is unable to work.

If you and your spouse are both retired (and your children, if any, are grown and gone) and there is still sufficient retirement income to support your lifestyle if either of you dies then you probably do not need any life insurance. Although your grown children may feel otherwise, you are not expected to provide an income or an inheritance for them.

Note: Life insurance death benefits are typically not subject to income tax (to recipients) but may be subject to estate taxes (to the estate).

There are two basic types of life insurance: whole life and term life. Purchasing whole life insurance is strongly discouraged. Mathematically, it is a poor investment. Any savings portion of a whole life premium is forgone if a death benefit is paid. If you currently have a whole life policy you should begin working to replace it with a term life policy. When the new term life policy is in place then cancel the whole life policy, but not beforehand. Term life is much less expensive than whole life because you are not paying any additional amount into the savings plan.

Whole life insurance does not fit in well with the philosophy promoted in the TruPlan Road Map. It is better to keep your investment plan separate from your insurance plan in order to maintain better control over each aspect and to be able to more easily calculate the costs and benefits of each. While you are still in debt you should not put any money (except to receive your company's matching contribution) into any type of investment plan, including whole life insurance. Instead, you should be funneling as much money as possible into paying down your debt.

Health Insurance

Health insurance is insurance that provides financial protection for medical expenses. To avoid financial ruin or at the very least crushing medical debt, it is essential to acquire health insurance for yourself and each member of your household that you support financially.

Depending upon the type of health insurance coverage and the benefits offered, health insurance can be very expensive. Policies offered through employer plans are usually the most affordable because many employers subsidize the health insurance premium. An employer-sponsored plan is usually, but not always, the best option for health insurance.

Most health insurance plans do not pay one hundred percent of medical costs. An insured person will usually be expected to pay a portion of the costs of medical care. The insured's portion may come in the form of co-pay, co-insurance, deductibles, or some combination of all three.

Co-pays are fixed dollar amounts that an insured must pay to their medical services provider at the time of each office visit or prescription purchase. Co-insurance is usually a percentage arrangement where the insurance company and insured each pay a portion of the cost of care. In a typical arrangement the insurance company will pay a much larger percentage of the cost than what the insured pays. In many plans the insurance company will pay eighty percent and the insured will pay twenty percent but the percentages vary by plan. Usually, but not always, the co-insurance arrangement comes into play only after a specified deductible amount is paid by the insured.

A deductible is a fixed dollar amount that an insured must pay toward incurred medical expenses before the co-insurance portion of coverage kicks in. In a low-deductible (higher cost) plan this amount may be one thousand dollars per year per family member. In a high-deductible (lower cost) plan this amount may be three thousand dollars or more per year per family member. Many plans include a cap that limits the number of family members that must meet the required deductible each year.

Unfortunately, most employer-sponsored health plans are not 'portable'. Portability is the concept that allows you to continue with your same plan regardless of your employment situation. If you leave a job voluntarily or involuntarily you may be eligible for COBRA coverage for eighteen months or longer after termination. Before leaving a job, investigate the cost of acquiring replacement health insurance coverage in the location where you will be living. Also, be sure to confirm your eligibility for a new plan before voluntarily giving up your old one.

Many people are unable to take advantage of a company-sponsored health insurance plan because their employer does not offer a health plan, or they are ineligible due to being part-time or temporary.

One option is a class of policies known as high-deductible policies. These policies provide limited benefits and come with high deductibles and premiums. If you have an employer-sponsored high-deductible plan then you may be able to take advantage of a Health Savings Account (HSA). Some employers offering HSAs make contributions to the account on your behalf. Contributions by employers and employees are not taxed. Account funds may be used to pay qualified medical expenses. The Affordable Health Care Act ("Obamacare") provides premium subsidies in some instances. Refer to *Appendix F – Online Resources* for health care-related links.

Other options for individuals with small children or medical disabilities may include programs such as Medicare/Medigap, Medicaid, or CHIP. Such programs are often funded by the federal government but are usually administered by state-run entities. Some of these plans are means-tested (premiums are based on income level).

Regardless of the source, it is important to obtain health insurance to protect yourself and your family. Carefully weigh the benefits provided under each available plan against the premiums to be paid in order to determine which offers the best value for your family.

Property Insurance

Property insurance, also known as casualty insurance, protects your property against theft, collision, fire, flood, hail, tornadoes, hurricanes, lightning, vandalism and a few other perils. Property insurance may also include liability and/or medical coverage, which protects you financially when you cause damage to someone else's property or when someone (other than you or your family) is injured while on your property.

The specific coverage provided by property insurance will vary by insurer. These variations often come in the form of written riders and exclusions which become a part of your policy. It is important to read the fine print when considering the purchase of property insurance. This is also true of any agreement or contract for service that you may enter into. You would do well to consult your wise counselors when evaluating insurance coverage. For individuals, there are three primary categories of property insurance: Homeowners, renters, and vehicle policies.

Homeowners' policies protect your personal residence (the dwelling you own and inhabit) and the contents within that dwelling. Depending on how your policy is written, your personal possessions may also be covered against loss, theft or damage even if they are not in your dwelling at the time of loss. Many options (riders) are available to custom-tailor your policy. Be sure to understand the options and costs associated with each.

If you have a mortgage (or other loan secured by the deed to your property) then you will normally be required by the lender to insure the property and to name that lender as a beneficiary. Lenders usually insist on this to protect their interests. Even if insurance is not required, it is always a good idea to insure your valuable property. Most people cannot afford to lose their house, automobile or other expensive assets due to theft, fire, flood, etc.

Renters' policies protect contents within a dwelling. The coverage is about the same as for a homeowner's policy, but the dwelling itself is not covered because the occupant has no financial interest in it. Renters' policies are less expensive than homeowners' policies since the value of the dwelling is not covered.

Insurance policies for vehicles can include several types of coverage. Covered vehicles can include automobiles, trucks, motorcycles, recreational vehicles (RVs), boats, jet skis, four-wheelers, etc. Policies may provide full coverage (repair or replacement cost for your vehicle), or liability only (repair or replacement of a non-owned vehicle that you have damaged). If you have a loan against your vehicle, you will probably be required by the lender to have full coverage insurance until the loan is paid in full.

Your vehicle policy may also include 'uninsured motorist' coverage. This coverage pays for damages to your vehicle by another person when that person does not have insurance coverage sufficient to pay for your damages. Many states require that vehicle owners obtain liability coverage for any owned vehicle but many drivers break the law by not acquiring the required coverage.

It is important that you always have adequate vehicle insurance. Think about how your life would be affected if you lost the use of one of your vehicles, particularly your automobile. How would you get to work? How would your children get to school? The inconvenience alone would adversely impact your life, not to mention the financial cost of having to replace that vehicle. How would you feel if you spent five years paying for a car, only to lose it due to an unexpected accident? How would you be affected if you had to spend the next five years paying for someone else's car and/or medical bills because you were uninsured and caused an accident?

Disability Insurance

Disability insurance provides coverage for individuals in the event they can no longer work due to medical reasons. Disability insurance covers loss of wages, not medical costs. Many employers offer disability insurance as an employee benefit. Both short- and long-term disability coverage plans usually have elimination periods. Elimination periods prevent the insured from being reimbursed for an initial period of loss (a form of co-insurance), typically three to six months. Benefits paid under disability insurance policies usually range from 40 to 60 percent of lost wages. Benefits typically cease being paid anywhere from six months up to normal retirement age. Be sure to review and discuss benefits, costs, and limitations with your wise counselors before signing up.

Long-Term Care

Long term care insurance provides coverage for individuals who become unable to completely care for themselves due to chronic illness or disability. This coverage pays for someone to provide needed help with skilled specialty medical services, or non-skilled activities, such as bathing, dressing, eating, taking medications, and light housekeeping. The care can be delivered in-home, in assisted living facilities or in nursing homes. Often this coverage makes the difference between an individual remaining at home or being forced to move to an assisted living or nursing home facility, which can be very expensive.

Long term care policies can be expensive and benefits can vary widely in features and cost. Such policies may not offer a sufficient payback for the premium payments that you will make. Be sure to carefully consider the benefits and costs and discuss with your wise counselors before committing to purchase a long term care policy. You must be sure you can continue to pay premiums over the long-term if you purchase this type of insurance.

Credit Life Insurance

Credit life insurance is a life insurance policy that is issued to pay the unpaid balance of a borrower's loan should the borrower die before the loan is paid. The value of the policy decreases as the loan balance decreases. Term life insurance rates are available at lower cost than credit life. Therefore, credit life insurance is not recommended. Purchase of credit life insurance cannot legally be required as a condition for approval of a loan.

GAP Insurance

Guaranteed Auto (or Asset) Protection (GAP) is a form of insurance that, in general, protects a borrower against loss due to accident or theft of a vehicle or other property item when the insurance settlement is less than the loan balance. This coverage is usually much more valuable early in the life of the loan when the loan balance is higher relative to the value of the insured item.

Travel Insurance

Travel insurance is a category of insurance that offers financial protection for trips involving airline flights, ocean cruises, and/or travel to foreign countries. Trip cancellation or interruption is one of the most common types of coverage. Medical expense and medical trauma transportation is another form of coverage. Lost or stolen baggage is also a commonly-offered coverage. Travel insurance can cost as much as five to ten percent of the cost of the trip so it may not be a good value depending on the circumstances.

Be sure to read and understand all of the coverage details, exclusions and exemptions stated in the policy beforehand. Generally speaking, you should decide whether you can afford to take the loss (self-insure) in the event that a trip is canceled due to weather, war, family illness or death, or other unforeseen circumstances. If you cannot afford to self-insure, then travel insurance may be appropriate.

Roadside Assistance

Roadside assistance is also a form of insurance. It provides assistance in the event that a subscriber has a vehicle breakdown and needs a tow, battery jump, door unlocked, gasoline, etc. Subscriptions may also give discounts on car rentals, lodging, etc.

Roadside assistance is not recommended. Instead, make sure your vehicle is roadworthy and monitor fuel, oil, and tire pressure levels before and during trips to minimize the likelihood of a breakdown requiring assistance.

Investment Protection

Insurance is a topic that many people may not consider when thinking about investing. Some forms of investing are often viewed as a high-risk activity, similar to gambling. However, there are some protections in place that provide significant benefits for most individual investors.

Banks may offer deposit insurance through the FDIC. Credit unions and savings and loan associations may offer deposit insurance through the NCUA. Investors in the stock and bond markets may be protected against fraud (but not against market losses) through the SIPC. The key word here is 'may' because some financial institutions may be exempt from these requirements. Financial institutions do fail from time to time so always verify that your financial institution provides federally-mandated deposit and investor insurance protection before establishing a business relationship. Refer to *Chapter 7 - Investing* for more information about investments.

Extended Warranties

Extended warranties are a type of insurance. Most retailers that sell vehicles, electronics and appliances also offer extended warranties. These warranties typically extend the warranty period offered by the manufacturer for an additional one to three years. Extended warranty providers are typically financially unrelated to either the seller or manufacturer, thus limiting responsibility for claims to the provider only.

Because extended warranties are expensive relative to the price of the merchandise and the potential benefits to be obtained, buying an extended warranty is discouraged.

Identity Theft Protection

Identity theft insurance is designed to protect consumers in the event that fraud is committed using the identity of the consumer. Several consumer advocacy organizations have studied the benefit plans of these policies and have concluded that this type of coverage is not worthwhile. Many of the safeguards offered by the policy vendors can be implemented directly by consumers with little or no cost. Refer to *Appendix I – Identity Theft* and *Appendix F – Online Resources* for more information on this topic.

This page intentionally left blank

6 - Transportation

"We are the first nation in the history of the world to go to the poorhouse in an automobile." - Will Rogers

Transportation is an important part of everyday living. Work, school, shopping, business appointments, recreational activities, etc. require that you be able to leave home and go to places where the activities occur.

Ideally, you would have multiple options to meet your transportation needs with the greatest convenience and the lowest cost. Most people, except perhaps those living in densely packed urban areas, consider an automobile to be a necessity and not a luxury. Overall, vehicles can be very expensive to own and operate. Vehicles lose their value over time and are a poor investment.

Affordability

You should only have a minimal amount of money tied up in vehicles. As a rule of thumb, you should never own vehicles for personal use that are collectively worth more than about half of your gross annual income. This would include the total market value of all vehicles you own, including recreational vehicles such as boats, motorcycles, campers, jet skis, snowmobiles, four-wheelers, trailers, etc.

Do not buy a car until you at least have your basic emergency fund in place and can also afford to purchase vehicle insurance. It is acceptable to pay your insurance premiums on a monthly basis, but it is often slightly less expensive to pay premiums quarterly, semi-annually, or annually.

Purchase Process

When shopping for a vehicle, be sure you are not overcharged. Go online to Kelly Blue Book (www.kbb.com) or similar web sites to determine what a fair price should be. Be sure to check out a vehicle's history using VIN number search sites. Some of these sites require a fee. Refer to *Appendix F – Online Resources* for links to vehicle fair market value and title search sites.

Some car dealers are eager to quote you a monthly payment amount but do not want to tell you the actual sales price of the car. Be wary of dealers like this. Know the maximum amount you can afford to spend, including taxes, transfer fees, and initial insurance payment before the shopping begins.

Be sure to carefully review the sales contract for hidden or excessive charges and fees before you sign. Take one of your wise counselors along with you when car shopping and never buy a car the first time you see it. Slow down and make sure your purchase is based on a financial, not emotional, basis.

Ensure that vehicle titles are kept up to date. The title must be transferred to the new owner any time a vehicle is sold, traded in, or given away. If this is not done the registered owner is still responsible for offenses associated with the vehicle. This would include parking tickets, toll violations, and possibly criminal activity. Penalties may also be assessed for failing to transfer title in a timely fashion.

Financing

Carefully consider the need to finance a vehicle. Use alternative transportation options, such as public transportation, car-pooling, etc. until you can pay cash. If no alternative transportation options exist, and if you must have transportation to get to and from your job, it may be acceptable to finance a cheap commuter car.

When considering a vehicle purchase, always research to find out the full cost of ownership, including repairs, insurance, depreciation, and fuel economy.

If you are in debt (except for a home mortgage) you should not own any recreational or other non-essential (non-commuter) vehicles. If you do, sell them because you can only afford to own an inexpensive vehicle that provides basic transportation to work or school. Your commuter vehicle should be worth very little, perhaps less than $2500. If it is worth more you should consider selling it and buying a cheaper one until your non-mortgage debts are paid off.

Review *Appendix F – Online Resources* for links to web sites to help you with vehicle purchasing and maintenance activities.

7 - Investing

"Dig the well before you are thirsty." – Viking Proverb

Investing can be defined as committing money or other assets in order to gain profitable returns in the form of interest, income, or appreciation of the value of the assets. In other words, investing is a form of lending. Investing is a very broad and complex topic. The mathematics, strategies, and technicalities of investing are too numerous to cover in a single book chapter or even an entire book.

Instead, the focus of this chapter will be to recognize the right reasons and time frames for individuals to begin investing, appropriate amounts to invest relative to an individual's current financial position and goals, and the selection of the types of investments that are in line with an individual's tolerance for risk. Refer to *Appendix F – Online Resources* for links to websites that provide more information on investment strategies.

Reasons to Invest

Gain is the fruit of successful investing. That fruit can be enjoyed immediately but in many cases it is preserved for future consumption, primarily during retirement years. In modern times the burden for retirement security is falling much more on individuals and much less on employers and government.

Employer-funded pension plans (more specifically, 'defined benefit plans') are quickly disappearing from company benefit offerings in an effort to shave costs and remain competitive in the global economic environment. At the same time, the federal Social Security system is in danger of being seriously scaled back over the next several decades due to the chronic inability of our elected leadership to properly manage the federal budget.

In the face of this new economic reality, the majority of individuals must now proactively plan for retirement, which usually means regularly setting aside a portion of income for the future. That set-aside, if managed properly, can grow nicely over a period of many years. The expectation is that when retirement comes there will be a 'nest-egg' large enough to meet or at least significantly supplement the cost of living during retirement. Retirement investment accounts will be covered in more detail later in the chapter.

Certainly there are other reasons to invest and create income. Many investors enjoy the challenge of making good investment decisions. Some investors prefer spending some or all of the extra income and having a higher standard of living, while still others wish to share the income with family members or to make charitable donations to worthy causes. Many investors do all of these things to varying degrees with their investment gains.

The Right Time to Invest

Looking back to the TruPlan Road Map, the right time to begin investing is when the emergency fund is fully in place and the investor is debt-free (except for the home mortgage). The fully-funded emergency fund should be sufficient to cover any emergencies and to protect your ability to continue contributing faithfully and regularly to the investment account.

Temporarily setting aside any philosophical arguments against debt, the mathematical argument for being debt-free before investing is very strong. Most lenders charge a relatively high rate of interest for borrowed money. It is virtually impossible to find a low risk investment that would pay a higher rate of return than the loan rate. Therefore it is always mathematically more profitable, and at zero risk, to invest dollars to eliminate all debt before beginning an investment program.

Making contributions to an investment account should continue without interruption until retirement begins. Contributions may continue even after retirement begins if there are other sources of income available that can be used to cover living expenses. A popular form of making contributions is known as dollar-cost averaging. By making regular contributions you will average out the normal up and down swings of the market. Trying to 'time' the market by investing at various points in time to capture market swings should only be practiced by professional money managers and is not recommended for individual investors.

At various times you may have extra money to invest but are in the process of deciding on where to invest it. While your research is underway you need a place to park your money. As with any money you possess, make sure you protect it by depositing it in a federally-insured financial institution. Confirm that your financial institution offers deposit insurance from a government-guaranteed agency such as the FDIC, NCUA, or SIPC.

The Right Amount to Invest

A general rule of thumb for making contributions to an investment account is fifteen percent of gross income per year. However, if you are starting late in life (beyond your 20's) then you must try to catch up by contributing a larger percentage of gross income. The exact amount would depend on your age, your current investment account balance and your retirement goals and other factors. While you are still working to pay off mortgage debt do not contribute more than fifteen percent towards your investment account. Refer to *Appendix F – Online Resources* for links to websites that have retirement calculators to assist with this analysis.

If completely debt-free, contribute every available dollar to your investment account. This is not to say you should live like a scrooge. It is alright to spend some income on creature comforts, philanthropy, and other life goals but you must strike a balance and realistically address your retirement needs at the same time. You should re-evaluate your retirement contribution level and investment strategy on an annual basis.

Some employers provide a benefit known as a 'matching contribution'. These benefits are offered through 'defined contribution plans' (commonly called 401K or 403B plans or something similar). If an employer provides a matching benefit it is a great idea to take full advantage of the match. After all, it is highly unlikely that you will find another completely risk-free investment opportunity that usually returns fifty to one hundred percent instantly!

Self-employed and other individuals with earned income can set money aside into retirement accounts known as Individual Retirement Accounts (IRAs). Self-employed persons may also utilize another, similar type of account called a Simplified Employee Pension (SEP).

Whether 401K or IRA or another plan type, the focus is on setting aside money on a regular basis and investing it in quality investments that offer reasonable returns with acceptable risks. Many of these 'alphabet-soup' plans are enticing because the federal government offers tax incentives by deferring income tax due on amounts set aside into these plans (subject to certain restrictions). Early withdrawals from retirement plans are usually subject to ten percent penalties plus the income tax due on the amount withdrawn. Generally speaking, it is never advisable to either withdraw money or borrow money from a retirement account.

The Right Way to Invest

As mentioned at the beginning of this chapter, investment strategy is a very broad topic. There are many ways to invest: Stocks, bonds, stock and bond mutual funds, treasury securities, real estate, commodities, certificates of deposit, and more. Each of these investment vehicles offers varying degrees of risk and return. Investors must take into account their needs for risk tolerance and diversification when deciding how to build an investment portfolio.

Research and consultation with your wise counselors and industry professionals is essential to gain a proper grounding in the ways to invest that are appropriate to each investor. Plan to spend a lot of time researching and learning about different investment philosophies. This chapter will only cover a few fundamental concepts of one of these investment options, stock and bond mutual funds. Stock and bond mutual funds are the most common and well-understood investment vehicles in the marketplace today.

It is difficult to emphasize how important it is to avoid the temptation to invest through a relative or someone else you know in the business without first seeking the advice of your wise counselors. Remember that investment advisers (even those that are your friends or relatives) make their living from selling financial products (including insurance) and services. Contrary to what they may say, most investment advisers are simply not in a position to give unbiased investment advice.

Start your investment portfolio by establishing a brokerage account with a medium- to large-sized nationally reputable firm that is SIPC-insured. All of the major brokerage houses offer online services for efficiency and convenience. Executing trades online is generally less expensive than relying on an investment adviser to make trades in your behalf. The brokerage house chosen should offer a large variety of mutual funds to select from. Each fund considered for investment should be investigated carefully. Federal law requires that brokerage firms provide a prospectus for each fund offered to aid investors in the decision-making process.

The mutual funds purchased or sold through an investment account should be 'no-load' (no fee for buying or selling funds). Brokerage houses also make money by charging monthly management fees, usually as a small percentage of the amount that is invested. Mutual funds employ professional money managers, accountants, and other staff to make decisions on what stocks and bonds to buy and sell, keep the paperwork in proper order, and provide account activity statements to the investors. Brokerage houses are required to publish information about the fees that are charged. Look for funds whose management fees are below one percent. Fees above one percent will consume a relatively large portion of investment gains and can significantly reduce what is available when retirement rolls around.

In general terms, invest in diversified stock and bond mutual funds available through the brokerage firm. Choose from funds that have an established and strong performance record relative to the market as a whole and that have been guided by a stable investment management team over a long period of time. Stock mutual funds are subject to risks, including possible loss of principal. Investments in bond mutual funds are also subject to risks, primarily because bonds are actually loans to the organizations issuing the bonds. Selection of specific funds is beyond the scope of this book and should be made in accordance with the advice of your wise counselors and your own research efforts. A fundamental rule of thumb is to decrease the level of risk as retirement draws near. This is because there is less time to recover from a down market when the time comes to begin withdrawals.

Avoid investing in individual stocks, commodities (i.e. gold, silver, pork bellies, etc.), junk bonds or other loans to individuals or businesses (except investment-grade bond mutual funds), life settlements, whole-life insurance policies, annuities (fixed or variable), or pledging or loaning your assets (or making personal guarantee) for someone else's loans. Be wary of any investment opportunity where the advertised rate of return is beyond what is available through conventional mutual fund investing. The old adage *"There is no such thing as a free lunch"* rings especially true with investments (Proverbs 13:11).

Always consider the risks along with any potential rewards. If you are unable to recognize and calculate the risks, then let that be your warning that you are stepping into unfamiliar territory and you should back away from the opportunity. For more specific advice on investing always start by consulting your wise counselors. If you do work with a professional investment adviser choose one that will work for a fixed fee, not a percentage of your portfolio.

This page intentionally left blank

Closing Thoughts

"Good judgment comes from experience, and a lotta that comes from bad judgment." – *Will Rogers*

Personal finance is such a broad subject that it is unlikely any one individual will become its master. Even though perfection is not possible, sufficient mastery can be obtained by diligent study and practice. The material that has been presented in this book should be considered an entry point and a framework for study and practice. May God bless you richly as you begin or renew your efforts to be a good steward of what He provides.

This page intentionally left blank

Appendix A – Financial Statement Template

"If we do not change our direction, we are likely to end up where we are headed."- Old Chinese proverb

Illustration A-1 Financial Statement Template (online at www.truplan.org)

Statement of Financial Position	
As of Date	
Asset Description	**Market Value or Account Balance**
Cash	
Checking	
Savings	
Emergency fund	
Vehicle 1	
Vehicle 2	
IRA accounts	
401K accounts	
Residence	
Jewelry	
Furniture, appliances, clothing, etc	
Other assets	
Total Assets	
Liability Description	**Account Balance**
Unpaid utility bills	
Unpaid rent/lease payment	
Credit card 1 – name:	
Credit card 2 – name:	
Credit card 3 – name:	
Vehicle loan 1 – name:	
Vehicle loan 2 – name:	
Medical bills	
Student loans	
Other debt 1 – name:	
Other debt 2 – name:	
Total Liabilities	
Net Worth (Assets minus Liabilities)	

Appendix B – Budget Template

"It's clearly a budget. It's got a lot of numbers in it." - George W. Bush

Illustration B-1 Budget Template (online at www.truplan.org)

Budget Month/Yr		Net Cash Flow (Income – Expense) Amount must be greater than zero.	
Earned Income		**Category**	**Amount**
Salaries, wages (net amount after taxes)		Regular earnings – full-time employment	
		Overtime pay	
		Bonuses	
		Home-based / part-time earnings	
Total Earned Income			
Misc. Income		**Category**	**Amount**
		Tax refunds (federal, state, and local)	
		Gifts, inheritance and other windfalls	
		Refunds and reimbursements	
		Transfers from savings	
		Other income	
		Interest on bank deposits	
		Investment gains and dividends	
Total Miscellaneous Income			
Assistance		**Category**	**Amount**
Entitlements		HUD / housing assistance	
		Food stamps	
		Utility subsidies	
		SSI payments	
Grants		Educational grants	
		Other grants	
Total Assistance - Entitlements and Grants			
Total Cash Inflow			
Expenses		**Category**	**Amount**
Food, Paper Goods		Groceries	
		Paper goods	
Clothing		Clothes	
		Laundry	
		Dry cleaning	
Personal Care		Haircuts, coloring	
		Manicures, pedicures	

	Personal hygiene / cosmetics	
Housing	Mortgage / rent payments	
	Maintenance (plumbing, roof, etc.)	
	Furnishings	
	Appliances	
	Lawn / garden	
	Home supplies	
	Improvements	
	Utilities – electric	
	Utilities – water	
	Utilities – gas	
	Phone – mobile	
	Phone – land line	
	Insurance	
	Storage building rental	
Transportation	Fuel	
	Regular maintenance (oil changes, etc.)	
	Personal property tax (license fees)	
	Parking, tokens, other commuter fees	
Debt	Car loan or lease payments	
	Mortgage payment (prin., int., escrow)	
	Credit card payments	
	Other consumer credit payments	
	Medical debt payments	
	Signature / payday loan payments	
	Loan payments to family and friends	
Savings	Emergency fund contribution	
	Home insurance & property tax fund	
	Automobile fund contribution	
	Furniture fund contribution	
	Vacation fund contribution	
	Investment fund contribution	
	College tuition fund contribution	
Entertainment	Hobbies	
	Vacation / travel	
	Dining out	
	Movie tickets	
	Movie / game rentals	
	Toys / games	
	Newspaper / magazine subscriptions	
	Club membership dues	

	Cable / satellite subscription	
	Internet service	
Philanthropy	Tithing	
	Giving	
	Volunteer (out-of-pocket expenses)	
Children	Day care fees	
	Babysitting fees	
	Child support payments	
	School tuition	
	Tutor / private lessons	
	School lunch	
	School supplies	
	Extracurricular: uniforms, fees, trips, etc.	
	Allowance (Proverbs 22:6)	
Medical	Medical insurance premiums	
	Prescription drugs	
	Vitamins	
	Doctor	
	Dentist	
	Optometrist	
	Therapist	
	Professional counselor	
	In home care	
	Other health-related expense	
Education (Adults)	Books	
	Tuition	
	Student parking and other fees	
Miscellaneous	Bank service charges and fees	
	General merchandise	
	Legal (fines, professional advice)	
	Income taxes (federal, state, local)	
	Other losses or discretionary expenses	
Total Expenses		

This page intentionally left blank

Appendix C - Scriptural References

"It is impossible to enslave mentally or socially a Bible-reading people. The principles of the Bible are the groundwork of human freedom." – Horace Greeley

This collection of scriptures is a broad, but not exhaustive, sampling of what the Bible says about money and possessions. All passages are from the New International Version (NIV) translation unless otherwise noted.

Table C-1 Scriptural References

Item	Category	Verse	Passage
1.	Blessing	Proverbs 10:22	"The blessing of the LORD brings wealth, and he adds no trouble to it."
2.	Blessing	Proverbs 16:3	"Commit to the LORD whatever you do, and your plans will succeed."
3.	Blessing	Isaiah 46:4	"Even to your old age and gray hairs I am he, I am he who will sustain you. I have made you and I will carry you; I will sustain you and I will rescue you."
4.	Blessing	Malachi 3:11	"I will prevent pests from devouring your crops, and the vines in your fields will not cast their fruit," says the LORD Almighty."
5.	Blessing	Matthew 6:21	"For where your treasure is, there your heart will be also."
6.	Blessing	1 John 5:14-15	"This is the confidence we have in approaching God: that if we ask anything according to his will, he hears us. 15 And if we know that he hears us--whatever we ask--we know that we have what we asked

			of him."
7.	Blessing	Acts 20:35	"…It is more blessed to give than to receive."
8.	Blessing	II Corinthians 9:7-8	"Each man should give what he has decided in his heart to give, not reluctantly or under compulsion, for God loves a cheerful giver. 8 And God is able to make all grace abound to you, so that in all things at all times, having all that you need, you will abound in every good work."
9.	Blessing	Philippians 4:6-7	"Do not be anxious about anything, but in everything, by prayer and petition, with thanksgiving, present your requests to God. 7 And the peace of God, which transcends all understanding, will guard your hearts and your minds in Christ Jesus."
10.	Blessing	Philippians 4:19	"And my God will meet all your needs according to his glorious riches in Christ Jesus."
11.	Blessing	I Timothy 6:8	"But if we have food and clothing, we will be content with that."
12.	Blessing	James 4:14	"…You are a mist that appears for a little while and then vanishes."
13.	Blessing	Psalms 20:4	"May he give you the desire of your heart and make all your plans succeed."
14.	Stewardship	Proverbs 14:29	"A patient man has great understanding, but a quick-tempered man displays folly."

15.	Stewardship	Proverbs 21:5	"The plans of the diligent lead to profit as surely as haste leads to poverty."
16.	Stewardship	Proverbs 21:20	"In the house of the wise are stores of choice food and oil, but a foolish man devours all he has."
17.	Stewardship	Proverbs 24:27	"Finish your outdoor work and get your fields ready; after that, build your house."
18.	Stewardship	Proverbs 27:23	"Be sure you know the condition of your flocks, give careful attention to your herds;"
19.	Stewardship	Jeremiah 29:11	"For I know the plans I have for you," declares the LORD, "plans to prosper you and not to harm you, plans to give you hope and a future."
20.	Stewardship	Matthew 7:6	"Do not give dogs what is sacred; do not throw your pearls to pigs. If you do, they may trample them under their feet, and then turn and tear you to pieces."
21.	Stewardship	Luke 14:28-30	"Suppose one of you wants to build a tower. Will he not first sit down and estimate the cost to see if he has enough money to complete it? 29 For if he lays the foundation and is not able to finish it, everyone who sees it will ridicule him, 30 saying, 'This fellow began to build and was not able to finish.'"
22.	Stewardship	II Thessalonians 3:10	"For even when we were with you, we gave you this rule: 'If a man will not work, he shall not eat.'"

23.	Wise Counsel	Genesis 2:24	"For this reason a man will leave his father and mother and be united to his wife, and they will become one flesh."
24.	Wise Counsel	Mark 3:25	"If a house is divided against itself, that house cannot stand."
25.	Wise Counsel	Psalm 119:93	"I will never forget your precepts, for by them you have preserved my life."
26.	Wise Counsel	Psalm 121:2	"My help comes from the LORD, the Maker of heaven and earth."
27.	Wise Counsel	Proverbs 1:5	"let the wise listen and add to their learning, and let the discerning get guidance—"
28.	Wise Counsel	Proverbs 11:14	"For lack of guidance a nation falls, but many advisers make victory sure."
29.	Wise Counsel	Proverbs 16:9	"In his heart a man plans his course, but the LORD determines his steps."
30.	Wise Counsel	Proverbs 19:20-21	"Listen to advice and accept instruction, and in the end you will be wise. 21 Many are the plans in a man's heart, but it is the LORD's purpose that prevails."
31.	Wise Counsel	Proverbs 31:10-11	"A wife of noble character who can find? She is worth far more than rubies. 11 Her husband has full confidence in her and lacks nothing of value."
32.	Integrity	Proverbs 3:27-28	"Do not withhold good from those who deserve it, when it is in your power to act. 28 Do not say to your neighbor, "Come back

			later; I'll give it tomorrow"-- when you now have it with you."
33.	Integrity	Proverbs 11:1	"The LORD abhors dishonest scales, but accurate weights are his delight."
34.	Integrity	Proverbs 13:11	"Dishonest money dwindles away, but he who gathers money little by little makes it grow."
35.	Integrity	Proverbs 13:22	"A good man leaves an inheritance for his children's children, but a sinner's wealth is stored up for the righteous."
36.	Integrity	Proverbs 22:1	"A good name is more desirable than great riches; to be esteemed is better than silver or gold."
37.	Integrity	Proverbs 22:6	"Train a child in the way he should go, and when he is old he will not turn from it."
38.	Integrity	Matthew 5:40-42	"And if someone wants to sue you and take your tunic, let him have your cloak as well. 41 If someone forces you to go one mile, go with him two miles. 42 Give to the one who asks you, and do not turn away from the one who wants to borrow from you."
39.	Integrity	Colossians 3:23	"Whatever you do, work at it with all your heart, as working for the Lord, not for men,"
40.	Integrity	1 Timothy 5:8	"If anyone does not provide for his relatives, and especially for his immediate family, he has denied the faith and is worse than an unbeliever."

41.	Money	Psalms 50:10	"for every animal of the forest is mine, and the cattle on a thousand hills."
42.	Money	Proverbs 28:20	"A faithful man will be richly blessed, but one eager to get rich will not go unpunished."
43.	Money	Ecclesiastes 6:7	"All man's efforts are for his mouth, yet his appetite is never satisfied."
44.	Money	Matthew 6:24	"No one can serve two masters. Either he will hate the one and love the other, or he will be devoted to the one and despise the other. You cannot serve both God and Money."
45.	Money	I Timothy 6:10	"For the love of money is a root of all kinds of evil. Some people, eager for money, have wandered from the faith and pierced themselves with many griefs."
46.	Money	Hebrews 13:5	"Keep your lives free from the love of money and be content with what you have, because God has said, 'Never will I leave you; never will I forsake you.'"
47.	Borrowing / Lending	Psalms 37:21	"The wicked borrow and do not repay, but the righteous give generously;"
48.	Borrowing / Lending	Proverbs 11:15	"He who puts up security for another will surely suffer, but whoever refuses to strike hands in pledge is safe."
49.	Borrowing / Lending	Proverbs 17:18	"A man lacking in judgment strikes hands in pledge and puts

			up security for his neighbor."
50.	Borrowing / Lending	Proverbs 22:7	"The rich rule over the poor, and the borrower is servant to the lender."
51.	Borrowing / Lending	Ecclesiastes 5:5	"It is better not to vow than to make a vow and not fulfill it."
52.	Borrowing / Lending	Romans 13:8	"Let no debt remain outstanding, except the continuing debt to love one another, for he who loves his fellowman has fulfilled the law."
53.	Tithing	Genesis 28:22	"and this stone that I have set up as a pillar will be God's house, and of all that you give me I will give you a tenth."
54.	Tithing	Leviticus 27:30	"A tithe of everything from the land, whether grain from the soil or fruit from the trees, belongs to the LORD; it is holy to the LORD."
55.	Tithing	Deuteronomy 14:22	"Be sure to set aside a tenth of all that your fields produce each year."
56.	Tithing	Nehemiah 10:38	"...bring a tenth of the tithes up to the house of our God, to the storerooms of the treasury."
57.	Tithing	Malachi 3:8	"Will a man rob God? Yet you rob me. But you ask, 'How do we rob you?' In tithes and offerings."
58.	Tithing	Malachi 3:10	"Bring the whole tithe into the storehouse, that there may be food in my house. Test me in this," says the LORD Almighty, "and see if I will not throw open the floodgates of heaven and pour out so much

			blessing that you will not have room enough for it."
59.	Tithing	Matthew 23:23	"Woe to you, teachers of the law and Pharisees, you hypocrites! You give a tenth of your spices--mint, dill and cummin. But you have neglected the more important matters of the law--justice, mercy and faithfulness. You should have practiced the latter, without neglecting the former."

Appendix D – Glossary of Financial Terms

"I'm a great believer in luck, and I find the harder I work, the more luck I have." - *Thomas Jefferson*

Table D-1   Financial Terms

Item	Term	Definition
1.	401-K (plan)	A retirement savings plan offered by for-profit employers that allows workers to save for retirement by making tax-deferred contributions. In many cases the employer will match a portion of the employee contribution.
2.	403-B (plan)	A retirement savings plan offered by public education and certain non-profit employers that allows workers to save for retirement by making tax-deferred contributions. In some cases the employer will match a portion of the employee contribution.
3.	Annuity	A product sold by financial/insurance institutions that is designed to manage and invest funds from an individual and then, at a predetermined point in time, pay out a stream of payments to the individual. Annuities are generally designed to be a means for an investor to obtain a steady cash flow during retirement years. Fixed annuities are structured to provide a fixed payment amount. In contrast, variable annuity payment amounts can increase and decrease over time based on the performance of the underlying investments.
4.	Appreciation	The gradual rise in the economic value of an asset over time usually due to inflation or increased demand. Contrast with Depreciation.
5.	APR	An acronym for Annual Percentage Rate. The APR is the calculated annual cost of credit during the life of a loan. Nominal APR is based on interest only, while Effective APR is based on interest and fees.

6.	APY	An acronym for Annual Percentage Yield. The APY calculation is similar to an APR calculation, but includes the effect of compounding interest earned. APY is usually quoted instead of APR when a deposit is involved, as opposed to a loan.
7.	ARM	An acronym for Adjustable Rate Mortgage. An ARM is a loan whose interest rate changes periodically in response to movements in financial markets.
8.	Balloon payment	A lump sum due at the end of a loan with monthly payments.
9.	Bankruptcy	A legal status conferred to an individual or organization by a court order when that individual or organization is deemed unable to pay debts owed to creditors. All bankruptcy filings are processed through the United States Bankruptcy Court. A Chapter 7 bankruptcy filing is a basic liquidation of all debt for individuals. A Chapter 13 filing is a repayment plan for individuals. Other types of filings exist for business and other organizations.
10.	Beneficiary	A person or other legal entity that receives money or some other valuable benefit from another person. Beneficiaries usually receive money from life insurance policies or from the distribution of the assets of a deceased person's estate.
11.	Brokerage account	An account relationship between an investor and a brokerage firm that allows an investor to deposit funds with the firm and place investment orders through the firm. The investor owns the assets in the account while the firm manages the recordkeeping aspects for all transactions.
12.	CHIP	An acronym for Children's Health Insurance Program. It is a children's Medicaid program. Typically the annual premium is fifty dollars or less for all children in a family. Co-pays for doctor visits of $5 to $25 are common. Families enrolled in CHIP may not have any other medical insurance policies for the covered

		children.
13.	Closing	A meeting at which documents are signed to transfer property from a seller to a buyer.
14.	Closing costs	Amounts paid as part of the settlement agreement when real estate is transferred from seller to buyer during closing. Amounts paid can include mortgage loan fees, real estate commissions, interest points, title insurance, attorneys fees, etc.
15.	COBRA	An acronym for Consolidated Omnibus Budget Reconciliation Act (1985). It is a law passed by the U.S. Congress and signed by President Reagan that, among other things, mandates an insurance program giving employees the ability to continue health insurance coverage for a set time after leaving employment.
16.	Collateral	Assets such as a car title, savings account, or deed to a house which are pledged by the asset's owner as security for a loan. If the loan is not paid as agreed, the lender has a legal right to take possession of the collateral, sell it and use the sales proceeds to satisfy the borrower's obligation.
17.	Compound interest	When interest is charged on a loan or earned on a deposit, and is added to the loan or deposit, so that the amount added also accrues interest. The effect of charging or earning interest on interest is called compounding. Compounding increases the actual amount of interest charged or earned.
18.	Conventional loan	A mortgage loan that is not insured by any government agency (not insured by VA or FHA).
19.	Credit rating	An assessment provided by a credit bureau that summarizes the ability of a borrower to repay loans.
20.	Default	A technical term meaning a borrower can no longer meet the requirements of a loan agreement, such as the ability to continue making required monthly payments or to provide required insurance for loan collateral.

21.	Defined benefit plan	An employer-sponsored retirement plan where benefits are determined based on factors such as salary history and duration of employment. Investment risk and portfolio management are entirely under the control of the company.
22.	Defined contribution plan	A retirement plan in which a specific dollar amount or percentage of earnings is set aside each payday (or other interval) by an employee. A benefit occurs because the income tax on the employee's contribution is deferred until withdrawn. Another benefit arises if and when an employer agrees to match the employee's contribution amount. The match is typically dollar-for-dollar up to a certain percentage of employee gross income, say four or five percent.
23.	Depreciation	The gradual decrease in the economic value of an asset. Depreciation is typically measured relative to the estimated lifetime of an asset and can be used to help establish a current value for the asset or to provide a potential tax benefit to a business owing that asset.
24.	Diversification	A methodology that mixes a wide variety of investments within a portfolio. The concept is that varying kinds of investments, on average, will provide higher returns and lower risk than would having a single investment within the portfolio.
25.	DJIA	An acronym for Dow Jones Industrial Average. Also called the Dow Jones, or simply the Dow, it is a stock market index. The Dow shows how thirty large, publicly owned companies based in the United States have traded during a standard trading session in the stock market. It is among the most closely watched U.S. benchmark indices tracking targeted stock market activity.
26.	Equity	The difference between the value of an asset, such as a home or car, and the unpaid balance of all loans against that asset.
27.	Escrow	An arrangement between two parties for a neutral third party to impartially manage funds or documents as part

	agreement	of a transaction between the two parties.
28.	Escrow payment	Typically a portion of a mortgage payment set aside to pay annual taxes and insurance assessed against the property.
29.	FAFSA	An acronym for Free Application for Federal Student Aid. FAFSA is the document that most states and schools use as the basis to award financial aid to applicants. Refer to *Appendix F – Online Resources* for related links.
30.	FCRA	An acronym for Fair Credit Reporting Act. Refer to *Appendix K – Summary of Your Rights under the Fair Credit Reporting Act* for more information.
31.	FDCPA	An acronym for Fair Debt Collection Practices Act. Refer to *Appendix L – Summary of Your Rights under the Fair Debt Collection Practices Act* for more information.
32.	FDIC	An acronym for Federal Deposit Insurance Corporation. The FDIC is a United States government corporation that provides deposit insurance, which guarantees the safety of deposits in member banks, currently up to $250,000 per depositor per bank. Financial institutions that do not publicly display FDIC placards do not participate in this plan and depositor accounts are therefore at risk if the financial institution fails.
33.	FHA	An acronym for Federal Housing Administration. The FHA is a government agency that provides alternative funding sources for home buyers that do not meet the stringent requirements of most mortgage lenders.
34.	FICA	An acronym for Federal Insurance Contributions Act. FICA is a required payroll deduction based on the gross income on your paycheck. FICA is your contribution to the federal Social Security fund. For both employers and employees, the rate has historically been 6.20%.
35.	FICO (score)	An acronym for Fair Isaac Corporation, a publicly-traded corporation (ticker FIC) that created the first

		credit-scoring system. A FICO Score is a measure of a person's credit worthiness. Other credit-scoring systems exist but FICO is the most widely used. A FICO score is used by lenders, insurance companies, and other risk-taking enterprises to help determine the acceptable rate of return (loan interest rate, policy premium amount) for the risk involved.
36.	FINRA	An acronym for Financial Industry Regulatory Authority. FINRA is the largest independent regulator for all securities firms doing business in the United States. FINRA's mission is to protect America's investors by making sure the securities industry operates fairly and honestly.
37.	Fixed annuity	See Annuity.
38.	Fixed rate loan	A loan where the interest rate does not change over the loan period.
39.	FSA	An acronym for Flexible Spending Account (or Arrangement). An FSA is an employer-sponsored plan that permits employees to set aside a portion of earnings to pay for qualified expenses, most commonly medical expenses, or dependent care. FSA payroll deductions are exempt from payroll taxes. The major disadvantage of an FSA is that money set aside but not used during the plan year is forfeited by the employee.
40.	FUTA	An acronym for Federal Unemployment Tax Act, a payroll tax on employers that funds benefits paid to unemployed workers. Employees do not pay this tax.
41.	Gross income	Your total pay - income from your paycheck before taxes and other deductions.
42.	HSA	An acronym for Health Savings Account. An HSA is a medical savings plan that is paired with a high-deductible insurance plan. The amount contributed to an HSA by an employee and/or employer is tax-deferred and can be used to pay most, but not all, medically-necessary expenses. Unlike a Flexible Spending Account (FSA)

		plan, money contributed to an HSA does not have to be spent by the end of the plan year.
43.	Identity theft	A form of fraud perpetrated by using another person's identity. Refer to *Appendix I – Identity Theft* for more information.
44.	Insurance	A form of risk management that is used to hedge against the risk of potential loss. Refer to *Chapter 5 - Insurance* for more information.
45.	IRA	An acronym for Individual Retirement Account. An IRA is a financial tool used by individuals to segregate funds for retirement savings and investing. Types of IRAs include Traditional IRAs, Roth IRAs, SIMPLE IRAs and SEP IRAs. Traditional and Roth IRAs are established by individual taxpayers. Contributions to a Traditional IRA may be tax deductible depending on income, tax filing status and coverage by an employer-sponsored plan. Roth IRA contributions are not tax-deductible. SEP IRAs and SIMPLE IRAs are retirement plans established by employers (and self-employed persons) which allow contributions by both employers and individuals.
46.	Life settlement	A form of investing involving the selling of a person's life insurance policy to a third party (typically an institution) for a onetime payment. The purchaser(s) then become the beneficiaries of the policy and pay the premiums. Fractional investment shares are often sold to individual investors.
47.	Load	Fees and/or sales commissions charged to an investor by a brokerage firm to buy or sell investment funds in behalf of the investor. Contrast with a 'No-Load' fund, which means no load is charged on the transaction.
48.	Medicaid	A health program for individuals and families with low incomes and resources. The program is managed by the states but is jointly funded by federal and state governments. Recipients must be U.S. citizens, permanent legal residents, or refugees. Beneficiaries

		include low-income adults, their children, and people with specific disabilities.
49.	Medicare	Medicare is the federal health insurance program for senior citizens age 65 and over. Medicare premiums are a required payroll deduction based on the gross income on an employee's paycheck. For employers and employees, the rate is 1.45% each. The rate for self-employed persons is 2.90%.
50.	Medigap	A type of insurance for medical expenses not covered under Medicare. Medigap policies, sold by private insurance carriers, provide supplemental health insurance coverage.
51.	MIP	An acronym for Mortgage Insurance Premium. MIP is mandated on FHA loans for borrowers that cannot meet the minimum equity requirement. The premiums collected are used to offset FHA's large losses due to mortgage defaults.
52.	NASDAQ	An acronym for National Association of Securities Dealers Automated Quotations. The NASDAQ is the largest stock exchange in terms of volume traded and market share in the world. It was the first stock market in the United States to start trading online.
53.	NCUA	An acronym for National Credit Union Administration. The NCUA is a US federal agency that supervises and charters federal credit unions and also insures savings in federal and most state-chartered credit unions. The National Credit Union Share Insurance Fund (NCUSIF) provides this insurance. Customer deposits held at credit unions and savings and loan associations that do not publicly display the NCUSIF placards are uninsured and are therefore at risk if the financial institution fails.
54.	Net income	Your net pay – income from your paycheck after all taxes, health care premiums, retirement savings plan and other deductions.

55.	No-load	See Load.
56.	Non-performing	A non-performing loan is a loan that is in default or close to being in default (according to the terms of the loan contract). Many loans become non-performing when payments of interest and principal are past due by 90 days or more, or there are other good reasons to doubt that payments will be made in full.
57.	Payroll deductions	Amounts withheld from a paycheck. Deductions are typically made from the employee's check for federal, state, and local income tax, Social Security (FICA) tax, Medicare tax, company retirement plan contributions, company-sponsored health and life insurance premiums, transfers to financial institutions for savings, etc. Not all state and local governments assess income tax (or collect income tax withholding).
58.	Personal finance	The application of the principles of effective money management to the financial decisions made by a person or family. Such decisions impact how earning, budgeting, saving, and spending patterns occur over time.
59.	PITI	An acronym for Principal, Interest, Taxes, and Insurance. The term refers to the full amount of a mortgage payment when all of these items are included.
60.	Prospectus	A document that provides information about an investment fund in a standardized format. Federal law requires investment brokers to provide prospectuses for each fund offered.
61.	Regulation E	A Federal Reserve Bank regulation protecting consumers that have been defrauded in electronic transfer transactions when the fraud is reported promptly. Refer to the Remediation section of *Appendix I – Identity Theft* for more information.
62.	ROI	An acronym for Return On Investment. ROI is a measure used to evaluate the efficiency of an investment. ROI is also used during the selection process to compare

		the returns of various investment opportunities. The formula used to calculate ROI is: (Gain [price when sold] – Cost [price when purchased]) divided by Cost [price when purchased]. The calculation result is usually expressed as a percentage or ratio.
63.	Risk tolerance	The degree of uncertainty that an investor is willing to undertake in regard to a negative change in the value of his or her portfolio. Typically, a higher rate of return brings with it a higher risk. Investors closer to retirement age (or retired) generally desire less risk (more safety) and will accept a lower rate of return in exchange.
64.	S&P (500)	An acronym for Standard and Poor's 500, a stock market index. The stocks included in the S&P 500 are those of the largest 500 (by market capitalization) publicly held companies that trade on either of the two largest American stock market exchanges: the New York Stock Exchange and the NASDAQ.
65.	SEP IRA	An acronym for Simplified Employee Pension Individual Retirement Account. See IRA for more information.
66.	Short sale	When an asset is sold and the proceeds are less than what is owed to the lender for that asset. The borrower still owes the difference to the lender after the short sale is completed.
67.	SIMPLE IRA	An acronym for Savings Incentive Match Plan For Employees Of Small Employers IRA. See IRA for more information.
68.	SIPC	An acronym for Securities Investor Protection Corporation. The SIPC helps individuals whose money, stocks and other securities are stolen by a broker or put at risk when a brokerage fails for other reasons. The SIPC does not cover individuals who are sold worthless stocks and other securities or securities that fall in value due to normal market price swings. The SIPC does not cover failures of banks, credit unions, or savings and loan associations (see FDIC, NCUA).

69.	Snowball (debt snowball)	A popular methodology used to pay off non-mortgage debt where the debt with the smallest balance is paid off first. Minimum payments are made on all other debt until the smallest balance is paid in full. The process is repeated with the next smallest balance, and so on, until all debt is paid.
70.	Take-home pay	See Net Income.
71.	Term-life (insurance)	A type of life insurance which provides coverage for a limited period of time (the term) but does not have any savings plan (cash value) associated with it. Term insurance periods typically range from five to twenty years. Level term simply means the payment amounts do not change during the term of the policy. Many employers provide term-life insurance at no cost to employees as a benefit.
72.	Variable annuity	See Annuity.
73.	Whole-life (insurance)	A type of life insurance that also has a savings plan built in. Whole-life insurance will have fixed or variable premium payments (paid over a whole lifetime). Other names for types of whole life insurance include universal life, variable universal life, endowment, and cash surrender life.
74.	Withholding (tax withholding)	Total amount withheld from a paycheck for federal, state, or local income taxes.

This page intentionally left blank

Appendix E - Compound Interest Chart

"The most powerful force in the universe is compound interest" – Albert Einstein

This chart graphically demonstrates the power of compound interest. This example uses an original investment amount of $10,000.00 accruing interest at six percent over twenty years. Simple interest earnings on that investment is $12,000.00. Interest earned using a compound interest formula is $22,071.00, an increase of nearly 84 percent!

Figure E-1 Effects of Compound Interest

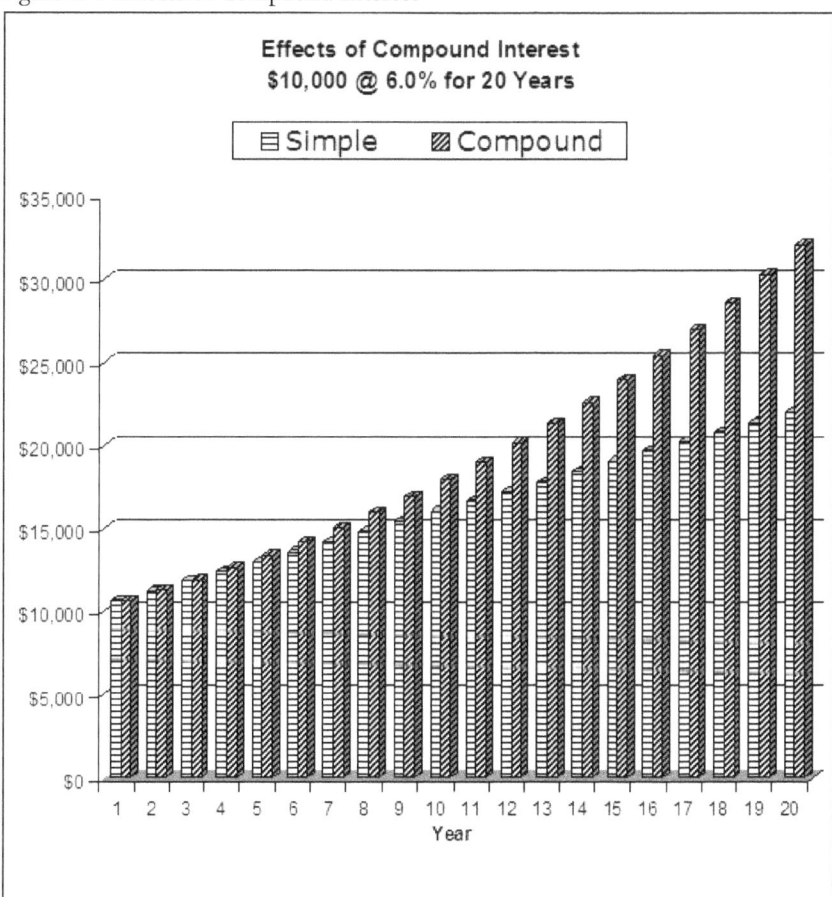

This page intentionally left blank

Appendix F - Online Resources

"Always bear in mind that your own resolution to succeed is more important than any one thing." - Abraham Lincoln

This table of hyperlinks will lead you to web sites that provide useful financial information. All sites listed provide some or all of their content for free. Some sites offer additional content on a paid subscription basis. Check the online listing at www.truplan.org for the most current information.

Table F-1 Hyperlinks

Item	Category	Name / Link	Description
1.	Credit	Annual Credit Report www.annualcredit report.com	The Fair and Accurate Credit Transactions Act (FACT Act) was signed into law in December 2003. The FACT Act, a revision of the Fair Credit Reporting Act, allows consumers to get one free comprehensive disclosure of all of the information in their credit file from each of the three national credit reporting companies once every 12 months through a Central Source. This is the official site.
2.	Credit	FTC Consumer Information http://www.ftc.gov /bcp/menus/cons umer/credit /debt.shtm	Federal government-sponsored site providing a list of resources for consumers with debt. Topics covered include bankruptcy, credit counseling services, debt collection agencies, credit repair, and consumer rights.
3.	Credit	Fair Credit Reporting Act	Summary of your rights Under the Fair Credit Reporting Act as

		Summary www.ftc.gov/bcp /edu/pubs/cons umer/credit/cre3 5.pdf	it appears on the Federal Trade Commission web site.
4.	Credit	Fair Debt Collection Practices Summary www.ftc.gov/bcp /edu/pubs/cons umer/credit/cre1 8.shtm	Summary of your rights Under the Fair Debt Collection Practices Act as it appears on the Federal Trade Commission web site.
5.	Fraud	Angie's List www.angieslist.com	User reviews of businesses by location and category. Note: This site requires a paid subscription.
6.	Fraud	Better Business Bureau www.bbb.org	Resource site for objective, unbiased information on businesses. BBB provide a network of national and local operations that monitor and take action on thousands of business issues affecting consumers.
7.	Fraud	Be Safe RX www.fda.gov/bes aferx	Federal government-sponsored site providing information about web sites selling prescription drugs.
8.	Fraud	Delivering Trust www.deliveringtr ust.com	U.S. Postal Service website for fraud education and prevention information.
9.	Fraud	Loan Modification	This national public education web site empowers homeowners

		Scam Alert http://www.loan scamalert.org/	to protect themselves against loan modification scams, find trusted help and report illegal activity to authorities.
10.	Fraud	Ripoff Report www.ripoffreport .com	Scams, product recalls, reviews and other timely consumer information.
11.	Fraud	Yelp www.yelp.com	User reviews of businesses by location and category.
12.	Health Care	Diseases and Conditions www.mayoclinic.c om/health-information	Comprehensive guide provided by the Mayo Clinic on diseases and conditions. The site includes both indexes and search engines to find definitions, symptoms, causes, risk factors, complications, tests, diagnoses, treatments, drugs, home remedies and healthy living tips.
13.	Health Care	Health Care Blue Book www.healthcarebl uebook.com	A free consumer guide to help you determine fair prices in your area for healthcare services such as surgery, hospital stays, doctor visits, medical tests and much more.
14.	Health Care	Hospital Compare www.medicare.gov /hospitalcompare	Hospital Compare is an official government site that has information about the quality of care at over 4,000 Medicare-certified hospitals across the country. Use this site to find hospitals and compare the quality of their care.
15.	Health Care	Insure Kids Now	A government-sponsored site

		www.insurekidsn ow.gov	that provides information about Medicaid and CHIP services for families who need health insurance coverage. These programs are designed to be affordable for families who are not able to afford health insurance coverage in the private market or do not have coverage available to them.
16.	Health Care	Health Care.gov www.healthcare.gov	Federal site for finding health insurance and premium subsidies. ("ObamaCare").
17.	Health Care	Medicaid www.medicaid.gov	Official U.S. Government for information about how you and your family may qualify for free or low-cost health insurance coverage through Medicaid or the Children's Health Insurance Program (CHIP).
18.	Health Care	Medicare http://www.medic are.gov	Official U.S. Government site for the latest information on Medicare enrollment, benefits, finding Medicare-affiliated doctors and other health-care providers, hospitals, suppliers and plans. Medicare is a health insurance program for people age 65 or older, people under age 65 with certain disabilities, and people of all ages with End-Stage Renal Disease.
19.	Health Care	WebMD www.webmd.com	WebMD provides valuable health information, tools for managing health, and support to those who seek information.

			WebMD also offers credible and in-depth medical news, features, reference material, and online community programs.
20.	Investing	Broker Check www.finra.org/br okercheck	Research page providing background information on registered brokers and investment representatives.
21.	Investing	FINRA www.finra.org	Financial Industry Regulatory Authority (FINRA) is the largest U.S. investor protection agency. This site offers articles, interactive tools, alerts and other resources to help protect investors.
22.	Investing	Fund Analyzer apps.finra.org/fu ndanalyzer/1/fa.a spx	FINRA Investment fund analyzer provides information on over 18,000 funds.
23.	Investing	Municipal Securities Rulemaking Board www.msrb.org	The Municipal Securities Rulemaking Board (MSRB) promotes transparency and education for investors and other parties involved in municipal securities transactions.
24.	Investing	SEC for Seniors www.sec.gov/inves tor/seniors.shtml	Securities and Exchange Commission site that provides investment advice for seniors entering retirement.
25.	Legal	Nolo www.nolo.com	Legal forms and information for do-it-yourselfers, including low-cost online wills.
26.	Money	Consumer Action	Online version of The

		Management	Handbook http://www.usa.go v/topics/consumer /consumer-action-handbook.pdf	Consumer Action Handbook (PDF document). Contains general advice on shopping for goods or services, what to watch for when buying a car or home, ways to prevent identity theft, tips to understand credit, and how to resolve problems after a purchase. Includes contact information for filing consumer complaints with consumer organizations, corporations, trade associations, Better Business Bureaus, and government agencies.
27.	Money Management	Mint http://www.mint.c om/		Free web application that tracks your expenses, keeps a budget, and links to your financial accounts to provide an up-to-date picture of your financial situation. Note: Does not support all financial institutions.
28.	Money Management	Money Matters www.ftc.gov/bcp /edu/microsites/ moneymatters/in dex.html		Federal Trade Commission site that provides tips on money management, fraud and other personal finance topics.
29.	Money Management	My Money www.mymoney.gov		Federal government-sponsored site dedicated to teaching the basics about financial education. Also provides calculators for financial planning, retirement planning and starting a small business.
30.	Money Management	The Dollar Stretcher		The Dollar Stretcher, run by a former financial planner, features tips on dozens of ways

		www.stretcher.com	to save money.
31.	Philanthropy	Charity Navigator www.charitynavigator.org	Site that provides evaluations about the financial health, accountability and transparency of America's largest charities.
32.	Philanthropy	Tax Information for Charities & Other Non-Profits www.irs.gov/charities	Internal Revenue Service site that provides a searchable list of tax-exempt organizations and related information.
33.	Search	Bing www.bing.com	Online reference that provides links to information on almost any topic.
34.	Search	Google www.google.com	Online reference that provides links to information on almost any topic.
35.	Search	Wikipedia www.wikipedia.com	Online reference that provides links to information on almost any topic.
36.	Seniors	Dough Rollers www.doughroller.net/retirement-planning/online-retirement-calculators	This web page contains links to several retirement planning calculators.
37.	Seniors	Eldercare Locator www.eldercare.gov	Federal government-sponsored site connecting you to services for older adults and their families.
38.	Seniors	Family Caregiver Alliance	Web site for Family Caregiver Alliance, a resource for family caregivers.

		www.caregiver.or g/caregiver/jsp/h ome.jsp	
39.	Seniors	Medicare Rights Center www.medicarerig hts.org	Non-profit consumer group that helps Medicare beneficiaries navigate the complex enrollment and benefits system.
40.	Seniors	My Social Security www.socialsecurity. gov/mystatement	Social Security Administration web page that provides social security statement information. The statement is no longer mailed to younger contributors.
41.	Seniors	National Clearinghouse for Long Term Care Information http://www.usa.g ov/Topics/Senio rs.shtml	U.S. Department of Health and Human Services website that provides information and resources to help plan for long-term care needs. The site helps consumers to understand what long-term care is, how and where to get information and services, and how to pay for services.
42.	Seniors	Senior Citizens Resources www.usa.gov/Topi cs/Seniors.shtml	Federal government-sponsored site providing a variety of resources for seniors on topics including retirement planning, housing and health.
43.	Seniors	Social Security Administration www.socialsecurit y.gov	Social Security Administration site providing answers to frequently asked questions about Social Security and factors that can affect your benefits.
44.	Seniors	Social Security Custom Benefit	Social Security Administration web page that provides an estimate of your social security

		Calculator www.socialsecurity.gov/estimator	benefit based on your actual earnings record and desired retirement date.
45.	Seniors	Social Security Quick Benefit Calculator www.socialsecurity.gov/OACT/quickcalc	Social Security Administration web page that provides a quick estimate of your social security benefit based on your desired retirement date.
46.	Student Aid	Office of Federal Student Aid www.fafsa.ed.gov	Federal government-sponsored site that provides grants, loans, and work-study funds for college or career school. The organization informs students and families of the availability of federal student aid programs. The primary process for applying for and receiving aid from those programs utilizes the Free Application for Federal Student Aid (FAFSA). FAFSA applications are accepted and processed through this site.
47.	Taxes	Filing Information for Individuals www.irs.gov/Filing/Individuals	Federal government-sponsored web page provides information about filing federal income tax returns online at no charge.
48.	Taxes	Internal Revenue Service www.irs.gov	Internal Revenue Service site provides down-loadable tax forms and information about federal income tax. You can also file your tax return online at little or no cost (if income is below a certain level) and receive your refund much faster

			than by mailing your tax return. Much less expensive than using tax return businesses that offer "Instant Refund" services.
49.	Transportation	AutoCheck www.autocheck.com	Web site that searches by VIN number for vehicle history such as reported stolen, salvage or flood titles, accident reports, accurate mileage, etc. Reports are not all-inclusive and do not indicate a problem-free vehicle. This is a fee-based service.
50.	Transportation	CarFax www.carfax.com	Web site that searches by VIN number for vehicle history such as reported stolen, salvage or flood titles, accident reports, accurate mileage, etc. Reports are not all-inclusive and do not indicate a problem-free vehicle. This is a fee-based service.
51.	Transportation	Edmunds www.edmunds.com	Web site providing market value, reviews and other information for all makes and models of vehicles.
52.	Transportation	Kelly Blue Book www.kbb.com	Web site providing market value, reviews and other information for all makes and models of vehicles.
53.	Transportation	National Insurance Crime Bureau www.nicb.org	Web site that searches by VIN number for vehicles reported stolen (unrecovered), or salvage or flood titles. Reports are not all-inclusive and do not indicate a problem-free vehicle. This is a free service.

Appendix G - Money-Saving Tips

"The measure of who we are is what we do with what we have." - Vince Lombardi

Table G-1 Money-Saving Tips

Item	Category	Tip
1.	General	Learn the difference between needs and wants.
2.	General	Avoid making impulse purchases. Make a shopping list and stick to it.
3.	General	Always look for sales on items you plan to buy.
4.	General	Comparison shop whenever possible.
5.	General	Shop at consignment and thrift stores.
6.	General	Keep a minimal amount of money in your wallet.
7.	General	Ask for a discount if purchasing with cash instead of a credit card.
8.	General	Buy generic instead of name-brand products when possible.
9.	General	Do not purchase extended warranties on vehicles, electronics, or appliances.
10.	General	Consider using Co-op buying to share costs with neighbors. Be sure to carefully weigh the cost of any required Co-op membership dues relative to the savings expected.
11.	General	Write down all out-of-pocket spending (coffee, etc.) to see where/how other cuts can be made. You should always do this when starting a budget program to see where money is spent.
12.	General	Stop supporting others (excluding your minor children) if you have non-mortgage debt.

13.	General	Search for less-expensive daycare. Consider sharing in-house caregivers with other families.
14.	General	Spend less on education (community college vs. university, public vs. private, get grants). Be wary of scammers promoting educational programs that promise quick riches and high-paying jobs after short-term schooling. Always research and check references for these types of offers.
15.	General	Check with your employer's HR/Benefits department for wellness benefits, transit reimbursement, retail discounts, gym membership and childcare subsidies, flexible spending accounts, etc.
16.	General	Be careful not to overspend on gifts. Use your imagination and skills to create home-made gifts for holiday, birthday, and other special occasions.
17.	Food	Buy drinks and snacks from grocery stores instead of vending machines and convenience stores.
18.	Food	Brew your own coffee instead of purchasing it at StealBucks.
19.	Food	Prepare meal plans and grocery lists in advance to reduce eating in restaurants.
20.	Food	Buy your planned list of grocery items from stores that price-match and accept coupons. Clip coupons (printed and online) at least for items that you buy frequently.
21.	Food	Consider joining a food warehouse club if you spend a large portion of your income on groceries. Be sure to carefully weigh the cost of any required membership dues relative to the savings expected.
22.	Food	Eat out only for special occasions and drink water when you do. Take restaurant leftovers home.
23.	Food	Take lunch to work (learn to love leftovers).

24.	Food	When preparing ingredients (i.e. chopping vegetables) for meals plan ahead to use some of those same items for other recipes and not just as leftovers. Many ingredients can be frozen without loss of taste or nutritional value.
25.	Housing	Consider downsizing your home in size and price to save on interest, insurance, taxes, utility costs and upkeep (discuss with your wise counselors).
26.	Housing	Conserve energy. Do an energy audit (contact your local energy company for guidance) to find the best ways. Electronics represent five percent of household usage so plug electronic devices (including chargers) into power strips and turn them off when not in use. Lighting represents about ten percent of usage so save half of that on lighting energy by switching incandescent bulbs to compact fluorescent lamps (CFL) or light-emitting diodes (LED). Keep in mind that CFL and LED bulbs are more expensive so use these bulbs primarily in high-usage areas. Water heating is twelve percent of usage so switch the clothes washer from hot to warm water to cut energy usage by half. Do full loads in clothes and dish washers. Set the water heater to a maximum of 120 degrees. Wrap the water heater in an inexpensive thermal blanket. Air conditioning consumes twelve percent of home energy so set thermostats as high as possible (each degree saves three percent). Install inexpensive programmable thermostats. Close drapes or blinds during the day time. Use fans to spread cool air. Open windows at night instead of running the AC unit. The heating system uses thirty percent of home energy so seal all ductwork leaks and leaks around doors and windows. Upgrade to a high-efficiency (Energy Star) furnace if your system is old and you plan to stay in the home for several years.
27.	Housing	Repairs to heating, cooling, plumbing or other systems can be expensive. Consider getting two or more written estimates before permitting work to begin. However, do not base your choice of

		contractors solely on lowest bid. Refer to the "Home Repair and Remodeling" section in *Chapter 4 – Housing* for more information on contractor selection.
28.	Housing	Consider taking in a roommate to share expenses (but check references carefully beforehand).
29.	Transportation	Run several errands at a time to save fuel.
30.	Transportation	Use a lower grade fuel if your vehicle's owners manual allows it.
31.	Transportation	Change engine oil in accordance with manufacturer's recommendation. The interval for many modern vehicles is five to seven thousand miles, not three thousand as suggested for older vehicles.
32.	Transportation	Buy monthly passes for public transportation instead of buying individual tickets.
33.	Transportation	Switch to a vehicle that costs less to own and operate.
34.	Transportation	Vehicle repairs can be expensive. Consider getting two or more written estimates before permitting work to begin. Ask a mechanically-inclined friend for advice (if you have one).
35.	Transportation	Buy used cars in good condition instead of new and keep them at least ten years. New cars can lose up to half their value after three years.
36.	Transportation	Keep your tires inflated to the pressure recommended by the vehicle manufacturer for better fuel economy.
37.	Transportation	Wash your vehicle at home or at the do-it-yourself car wash instead of the drive-through.
38.	Entertainment/ Communications	Eliminate your subscriptions to cable/satellite TV, Netflix, satellite radio, etc.
39.	Entertainment/ Communications	Eliminate cell phones or land lines (check for early termination fees first) or cut down on cell phone usage and get a cheaper contract. Check the potential

		cost savings of using a prepaid service.
40.	Entertainment/ Communications	Switch to a lower-cost internet service provider (check early termination fees).
41.	Entertainment/ Communications	Do not renew newspaper and magazine subscriptions (use the internet and/or library instead).
42.	Entertainment/ Communications	Buy used audio/video equipment in good condition instead of buying new. Ask about existing warranty coverage but do not buy extended coverage.
43.	Entertainment/ Communications	Use the local library for free or cheap books, movies and music. Always remember to return items on time to avoid paying late fees.
44.	Entertainment/ Communications	Buy used CDs and DVDs at music stores, pawn shops, garage sales, etc. Do not buy movies if you will only watch them one or two times (rent instead).
45.	Entertainment/ Communications	Watch movies at home (using pre-owned DVDs or low-cost internet movie streaming services) instead of going out to movie theaters.
46.	Health Care	Give up or cut back on alcohol and cigarettes.
47.	Health Care	Drop gym memberships and exercise at home instead.
48.	Health Care	Use health fairs, local labs, or the CDC to find free or low-cost health screening services.
49.	Health Care	Reduce the cost of prescription medications by buying generic, using low-cost prescription programs offered by large retailers (i.e. Walmart, Target), split pills (only with your doctor's consent), and by searching the internet for other legitimate prescription cost-reduction programs.
50.	Insurance	Purchase health, home, and auto insurance with higher deductibles. Refer to *Chapter 5 – Insurance* for more information.
51.	Insurance	Drop collision and comprehensive insurance on

		clunkers. Refer to the "Property Insurance" section in *Chapter 5 – Insurance* for more information.
52.	Insurance	Switch from expensive whole-life insurance to inexpensive term-life insurance. Refer to the "Life Insurance" section in *Chapter 5 – Insurance* for more information.
53.	Finance	Move your checking account to a financial institution that offers free checking.
54.	Finance	Avoid using ATMs that will charge you a fee (consider using cash back from local stores that you regularly shop in).
55.	Finance	Refinance your home for a lower interest rate (discuss with your advisers and always evaluate the fees).
56.	Finance	Regularly review your credit card and bank statements for errors. Report problems immediately.
57.	Finance	Check your credit report regularly for errors, fraud and signs of identity theft. Federal law allows you to obtain one free credit report annually from each of the three primary credit reporting organizations (Experian, TransUnion, and Equifax). Refer to *Appendix I – Identity Theft* for more information.
58.	Finance	Pay bills early to take advantage of discounts for early payment (if offered). Pay on time to avoid late fees.
59.	Finance	Never write an insufficient or overdrawn check. The fees are almost always very expensive.
60.	Finance	Choose investment funds with lower management fees (typically one percent per year or less). Refer to *Chapter 7 – Investing* for more information.
61.	Finance	Use a computer software program to file your tax return instead of paying a preparer. Filing online is free for qualifying individuals at www.irs.gov.

Appendix H – Checkbook Management

"Give me five minutes with a person's checkbook, and I will tell you where their heart is." – Billy Graham

Many people use checking accounts to pay bills. Checking accounts can be beneficial because they provide fund safety, transaction tracking, and convenience. Many vendors, such as utility and insurance companies, offer to deduct recurring payments automatically from checking accounts. Taking advantage of this service reduces the amount of time spent each month paying your bills.

On the downside, financial institutions usually charge monthly service fees for the use of an account. Nearly all financial institutions levy significant fees against customers who write checks against insufficient funds (hot checks) or maintain overdrawn balances. Merchants also charge high fees to account holders for checks returned due to insufficient funds.

Because of these potentially significant costs, it is important that you do not allow your account to become overdrawn or to write checks when the money is not available in the account. The best way to stay on top of your account is to balance your checkbook each month when your account statement is made available to you.

Balancing your checkbook each month (also called bank or checkbook reconciliation) is straightforward and does not take much time. The process entails comparing how much money the financial institution says you have with how much your check register says you have. Some account holders do not use a check register, either because they have duplicate (carbon copy) checks or they use debit cards (keep those receipts).

On-line banking can be helpful too, but you must remember to account for outstanding items. If you know where you stand, you can recover from errors before disaster strikes.

Table H-1   Checkbook Reconciliation Steps

Step	Description
1.	Start by examining your statement and the transactions shown. Make sure all of your deposits (keep those bank-stamped receipts) were posted to your account and that no unauthorized charges were deducted. Although this step is not technically part of the reconciliation process it is a great time to check for problems. If anything unusual is detected report it to your financial institution immediately! You may not be reimbursed for your loss if you fail to report it in a timely fashion (usually within thirty days).
2.	Update your check register by entering any amounts that appear on your current statement that are not listed in your register. This might include checks or debit card transactions that you forgot to write down, interest earned, service charges deducted, etc. Be sure to update the ending balance in your check register by adding or subtracting each new entry to the running balance. Don't forget to follow up with the bank on deposits entered in your checkbook but not posted on your statement.
3.	In your check register, mark all transactions that are listed in your account statement. When you have finished, make lists of all items in your register that were not marked. Make separate lists for debits (checks, charges, etc.) and credits (deposits, interest credits). For convenience use the form usually printed on the back of your account statement.
4.	Using the ending balance as shown on the account statement, add the total of unposted credits listed in the previous step, then subtract the total of unposted debits listed in the previous step. This net amount represents your adjusted bank balance.
5.	Compare the adjusted bank balance to the ending balance in your check register. These two amounts should be equal. If the amounts do not equal then an error exists and you should repeat Steps 1-4 in an effort to find it. If you cannot find the error, seek the assistance of a knowledgeable friend (Proverbs 1:5) or ask your financial institution for help. If the amounts are equal, then congratulations! The adjusted bank balance and check register ending balance accurately represent the amount of money available for you to spend as of the reconciliation period ending date. Don't give up! The more times you reconcile the easier it becomes.

Appendix I – Identity Theft

"The only place success comes before work is in the dictionary." - Vince Lombardi

Identity theft is a form of fraud perpetrated by someone using another person's identity. Typically, an identity is stolen in order to obtain credit or other resources held in the victim's name. The victim can potentially be held financially liable for the perpetrator's actions. In addition, those who are defrauded by an identity thief may also suffer other adverse consequences such as lost time and damage to reputation.

Prevention

Do not give out your personal information over the telephone (if you did not initiate the call) or to visitors at your door. This rule applies even if the caller or visitor says they are a representative of a financial institution or other company that you do business with or if they are just attempting to 'verify' your information.

Personal information includes your birth date and identifying numbers for Social Security, Medicaid, driver licenses, credit cards, and bank account or other financial statements. Imposters may contact you and ask to verify one or more of these numbers. Remember that banks, credit card issuers, and other service providers that you do business with already have your account numbers and so there is no reason to give out this information.

Unsolicited e-mails may be fraudulent. Be especially careful about e-mails that offer credit services. Do not click on links in unsolicited emails. These links may send you to web sites asking for your personal information. This tactic is called 'phishing' (pronounced 'fishing') because an attempt is being made to obtain your personal information. If you want to transact business on-line, go directly to the site by typing in the web address (URL) directly into your browser. If necessary, search for a company's web address using one of the major search engines. Make sure you select a link that is legitimate for the company you are searching for and not a copycat link.

Never leave your bank account, credit card or other financial statements lying around your home or office where others can see them. Never leave personal information in your vehicle. Do not let anyone other than your spouse, tax preparer or wise counsel have access to them. Check your credit card bill(s), bank account(s) and other financial statements as soon as you receive them. Review them carefully and look for any unauthorized charges. Shred all of your unnecessary documents and mail, including junk mail.

Most organizations that you do business with do not need your social security number. Employers, financial institutions, and some government agencies must have your social security numbers. For all other organizations, try providing your own nine-digit number (starting with 000, which is not used by the government). Carry your Medicare card only for planned doctor/hospital visits and carry your Social Security card only for visits to Social Security offices.

Keep all of your account numbers and related contact telephone numbers handy in case your credit card or other personal information is stolen. Keep this contact information separate from your wallet, purse or statements in case they are stolen.

Never use obvious passwords such your mother's maiden name, your children's names, parts of your social security numbers, your street address number, or birth dates. Never write your passwords or PIN numbers on anything that you carry in your purse or wallet. Use "strong" passwords (10 or more characters in length and including a mix of upper- and lower-case letters, numbers, and special characters such as # or $) and uncommon PIN numbers. Use "pass phrases" instead of passwords to make memorization easier and passwords harder to crack. Be sure to use current antivirus software on your computers.

Lock your smart phones, tablets, and other computing devices with a pass code/PIN number to prevent unauthorized access to your information.

Have your name removed from mailing lists for pre-approved credit card offers by visiting www.optoutprescreen.com. Stop other junk mail at www.dmachoice.com. Many banks and credit card issuers can provide free alerts for unusual account activity.

Formally close out any old credit card accounts that are no longer in use. Freeze your credit report if you do not plan to apply for new credit, insurance or utilities in the near future.

Do not let mail or newspapers pile up while you are away from home. Use a locking mailbox or post office box.

Remediation

You need to know what steps to take if you suspect or know that someone has stolen your personal information or has made unauthorized transactions on any of your accounts. It is very important to take immediate action in order to minimize the damage that may result.

If you suspect or know that someone has fraudulently obtained your personal information, you should assume an attempt will be made to use the information to defraud you. Federal law gives you the right to obtain a free credit report from each of the three major credit bureaus once each year. Refer to *Appendix F - Online Resources* for a hyperlink to the official website that provides free annual credit reports from the three major credit bureaus. Suggestion: To minimize the time between reviews get one free report from a different one of those agencies every four months.

Exercise caution using any other web sites to obtain your "free" credit reports. Many web sites masquerade as 'official' free credit report web sites but will attempt to charge you a fee or enroll you in a recurring fee-based service. The main web sites for the three major credit bureaus also engage in this tactic so be sure to use the one and only truly free site.

If you have evidence that someone has stolen your identity then take the following steps immediately: Contact at least one of the bureaus and put a fraud alert (freeze) on your account; Close any accounts fraudulently accessed; File a police report; Report the theft to the Federal Trade Commission (www.ftc.gov).

Under federal law (Federal Reserve Regulation E, Sec. 205.6 - Liability of Consumer for Unauthorized Transfers), you are not responsible for more than $50 of fraudulent charges on your credit card, online banking, ATM or debit card but you must report the problem within two days to gain this protection. Your liability jumps to $500 on the third day. After 60 days you are responsible for the entire loss. Follow the instructions on your account statement to dispute all fraudulent charges. Always keep copies of all emails and letters that you send or receive related to the fraud. Write down any conversation details, name, date and time of all persons that you have spoken with (on the phone or in person) about the fraud.

This page intentionally left blank

Appendix J – Marriage Checklist

"All men make mistakes, but married men find out about them sooner" - Red Skelton

Say "I Do", but not "I Didn't Know"

If you're thinking of tying the knot, first make sure you and your beloved are, financially speaking, on the same page. Money disputes are the leading cause of divorce in the United States. Failure to communicate about financial issues contributes to conflict between couples. Be sure to set aside time on a regular basis to discuss finances.

Before the big day review and discuss the checklist shown on the next page together. Make sure you and your partner know each other's financial situation well and can come into agreement on money management philosophy.

In addition to financial issues, be sure that you and your intended are aligned on religious, political, and familial issues as well. Undertake per-marital counseling offered by your church.

Table J-1 Marriage Checklist

Item	Topic	Tip
1.	Talk all about it	Review each others financial documents. Pay stubs, recent tax returns, bank statements, credit card bills, loan agreements. Consider conducting criminal background checks if there is any concern about a person's background. Review each others credit report and credit score. Discuss how credit will be used in the marriage, if at all.
2.	Make it fit	Discuss the concept of budgeting and come to an agreement on how the budgeting process will occur and what the rules are. Prepare actual combined budgets together and practice conflict resolution.
3.	Coin toss	Decide who will be primarily responsible for paying the bills and managing the bank accounts.
4.	Murphy is coming	Discuss and agree on what constitutes an emergency and how emergencies will be paid for. Agree on how much money the emergency fund will contain and specifically how it will be filled (and refilled).
5.	I'm fweeee!!	Agree on how much you can spend on anything without having to get your spouse's approval.
6.	Hi honey, I'm home!	Discuss when and how many children the marriage will produce (God willing) and which, if either, spouse will stay home when the children start showing up. If children will be part of the equation be sure to discuss whether they will attend public or private schools and what religious doctrine they will be taught.
7.	What are friends for?	Discuss and agree on a policy for lending money to family or friends, or not. If you agree that you will (not advised), discuss how much interest to charge, the maximum amount you are comfortable loaning out, collateral, and repayment terms.

Appendix K – Summary of Your Rights under the Fair Credit Reporting Act

The federal Fair Credit Reporting Act (FCRA) promotes the accuracy, fairness, and privacy of information in the files of consumer reporting agencies. There are many types of consumer reporting agencies, including credit bureaus and specialty agencies (such as agencies that sell information about check writing histories, medical records, and rental history records). Here is a summary of your major rights under the FCRA.

For more information, including information about additional rights, go to www.ftc.gov/credit or write to: Consumer Response Center, Room 130-A, Federal Trade Commission, 600 Pennsylvania Ave. N.W., Washington, D.C. 20580.

You must be told if information in your file has been used against you. Anyone who uses a credit report or another type of consumer report to deny your application for credit, insurance, or employment – or to take another adverse action against you – must tell you, and must give you the name, address, and phone number of the agency that provided the information.

You have the right to know what is in your file. You may request and obtain all the information about you in the files of a consumer reporting agency (your "file disclosure"). You will be required to provide proper identification, which may include your Social Security number. In many cases, the disclosure will be free. You are entitled to a free file disclosure if:

- A person has taken adverse action against you because of information in your credit report;
- You are the victim of identify theft and place a fraud alert in your file;
- Your file contains inaccurate information as a result of fraud;
- You are on public assistance;
- You are unemployed but expect to apply for employment within 60 days.
- All consumers are entitled to one free disclosure every 12 months upon request from each nationwide credit bureau and from nationwide specialty consumer reporting agencies. See www.ftc.gov/credit for additional information.

You have the right to ask for a credit score. Credit scores are numerical summaries of your credit-worthiness based on information from credit bureaus. You may request a credit score from consumer reporting agencies that create scores or distribute scores used in residential real property loans, but you will have to pay for it. In some mortgage transactions, you will receive credit score information for free from the mortgage lender.

You have the right to dispute incomplete or inaccurate information. If you identify information in your file that is incomplete or inaccurate, and report it to the consumer reporting agency, the agency must investigate unless your dispute is frivolous. See www.ftc.gov/credit for an explanation of dispute procedures.

Consumer reporting agencies must correct or delete inaccurate, incomplete, or unverifiable information. Inaccurate, incomplete or unverifiable information must be removed or corrected, usually within 30 days. However, a consumer reporting agency may continue to report information it has verified as accurate.

Consumer reporting agencies may not report outdated negative information. In most cases, a consumer reporting agency may not report negative information that is more than seven years old, or bankruptcies that are more than 10 years old.

Access to your file is limited. A consumer reporting agency may provide information about you only to people with a valid need -- usually to consider an application with a creditor, insurer, employer, landlord, or other business. The FCRA specifies those with a valid need for access.

You must give your consent for reports to be provided to employers. A consumer reporting agency may not give out information about you to your employer, or a potential employer, without your written consent given to the employer. Written consent generally is not required in the trucking industry. For more information, go to www.ftc.gov/credit.

You may limit "prescreened" offers of credit and insurance you get based on information in your credit report. Unsolicited "prescreened" offers for credit and insurance must include a toll-free phone number you can call if you choose to remove your name and address from the lists these offers are based on. You may opt-out with the nationwide credit bureaus at 1-888-5-OPTOUT (1-888-567-8688).

You may seek damages from violators. If a consumer reporting agency, or, in some cases, a user of consumer reports or a furnisher of information to a consumer reporting agency violates the FCRA, you may be able to sue in state or federal court.

Identity theft victims and active duty military personnel have additional rights. For more information, visit www.ftc.gov/credit.

Table K-1 FCRA Contact Information

States may enforce the FCRA, and many states have their own consumer reporting laws. In some cases, you may have more rights under state law. For more information, contact your state or local consumer protection agency or your state Attorney General. Federal enforcers are listed in this table.

Type of Business	Contact
Consumer reporting agencies, creditors and others not listed below National banks, federal branches/agencies of foreign banks (word "National" or initials "N.A." appear in or after bank's name)	Federal Trade Commission: Consumer Response Center - FCRA Washington, DC 20580 1-877-382-4357 Office of the Comptroller of the Currency Compliance Management, Mail Stop 6-6 Washington, DC 20219 800-613-6743
Federal Reserve System member banks (except national banks, and federal branches/agencies of foreign banks)	Federal Reserve Board Division of Consumer & Community Affairs Washington, DC 20551 202-452-3693
Savings associations and federally chartered savings banks (word "Federal" or initials "F.S.B." appear in federal institution's name)	Office of Thrift Supervision

Federal credit unions (words "Federal Credit Union" appear in institution's name)	Consumer Complaints Washington, DC 20552 800-842-6929 National Credit Union Administration 1775 Duke Street Alexandria, VA 22314 703-519-4600
State-chartered banks that are not members of the Federal Reserve System Air, surface, or rail common carriers regulated by former Civil Aeronautics Board or Interstate Commerce Commission	Federal Deposit Insurance Corporation Consumer Response Center, 2345 Grand Avenue, Suite 100 Kansas City, Missouri 64108-2638 1-877-275-3342 Department of Transportation , Office of Financial Management Washington, DC 20590 202-366-1306
Activities subject to the Packers and Stockyards Act, 1921	Department of Agriculture Office of Deputy Administrator - GIPSA Washington, DC 20250 202-720-7051

Appendix L – Summary of Your Rights under the Fair Debt Collection Practices Act

Debt Collection FAQs: A Guide for Consumers

If you're behind in paying your bills, or a creditor's records mistakenly make it appear that you are, a debt collector may be contacting you.

The Federal Trade Commission (FTC), the nation's consumer protection agency, enforces the Fair Debt Collection Practices Act (FDCPA), which prohibits debt collectors from using abusive, unfair, or deceptive practices to collect from you.

Under the FDCPA, a debt collector is someone who regularly collects debts owed to others. This includes collection agencies, lawyers who collect debts on a regular basis, and companies that buy delinquent debts and then try to collect them.

Here are some questions and answers about your rights under the Act.

What types of debts are covered?

The Act covers personal, family, and household debts, including money you owe on a personal credit card account, an auto loan, a medical bill, and your mortgage. The FDCPA doesn't cover debts you incurred to run a business.

Can a debt collector contact me any time or any place?

No. A debt collector may not contact you at inconvenient times or places, such as before 8 in the morning or after 9 at night, unless you agree to it. And collectors may not contact you at work if they're told (orally or in writing) that you're not allowed to get calls there.

How can I stop a debt collector from contacting me?

If a collector contacts you about a debt, you may want to talk to them at least once to see if you can resolve the matter – even if you don't think you owe the debt, can't repay it immediately, or think that the collector is contacting you by mistake. If you decide after contacting the debt collector that you don't want the collector to contact you again, tell the collector – in writing – to stop contacting you. Here's how to do that:

Make a copy of your letter. Send the original by certified mail, and pay for a "return receipt" so you'll be able to document what the collector received. Once the collector receives your letter, they may not contact you again, with two exceptions: a collector can contact you to tell you there will be no further contact or to let you know that they or the creditor intend to take a specific action, like filing a lawsuit. Sending such a letter to a debt collector you owe money to does not get rid of the debt, but it should stop the contact. The creditor or the debt collector still can sue you to collect the debt.

Can a debt collector contact anyone else about my debt?

If an attorney is representing you about the debt, the debt collector must contact the attorney, rather than you. If you don't have an attorney, a collector may contact other people – but only to find out your address, your home phone number, and where you work. Collectors usually are prohibited from contacting third parties more than once. Other than to obtain this location information about you, a debt collector generally is not permitted to discuss your debt with anyone other than you, your spouse, or your attorney.

What does the debt collector have to tell me about the debt?

Every collector must send you a written "validation notice" telling you how much money you owe within five days after they first contact you. This notice also must include the name of the creditor to whom you owe the money, and how to proceed if you don't think you owe the money.

Can a collector keep contacting me if I don't think I owe any money?

If you send the debt collector a letter stating that you don't owe any or all of the money, or asking for verification of the debt, that collector must stop contacting you. You have to send that letter within 30 days after you receive the validation notice. But a collector can begin contacting you again if it sends you written verification of the debt, like a copy of a bill for the amount you owe.

What practices are off limits for debt collectors?

Harassment. Debt collectors may not harass, oppress, or abuse you or any third parties they contact. For example, they may not:

- use threats of violence or harm;
- publish a list of names of people who refuse to pay their debts (but they can give this information to the credit reporting companies);
- use obscene or profane language; or
- repeatedly use the phone to annoy someone.

False statements. Debt collectors may not lie when they are trying to collect a debt. For example, they may not:

- falsely claim that they are attorneys or government representatives;
- falsely claim that you have committed a crime;
- falsely represent that they operate or work for a credit reporting company;
- misrepresent the amount you owe;
- indicate that papers they send you are legal forms if they aren't; or
- indicate that papers they send to you aren't legal forms if they are.

Debt collectors also are prohibited from saying that:

- you will be arrested if you don't pay your debt;
- they'll seize, garnish, attach, or sell your property or wages unless they are permitted by law to take the action and intend to do so; or
- legal action will be taken against you, if doing so would be illegal or if they don't intend to take the action.

Debt collectors may not:

- give false credit information about you to anyone, including a credit reporting company;
- send you anything that looks like an official document from a court or government agency if it isn't; or
- use a false company name.

Unfair practices. Debt collectors may not engage in unfair practices when they try to collect a debt. For example, they may not:

- try to collect any interest, fee, or other charge on top of the amount you owe unless the contract that created your debt – or your state law – allows the charge;
- deposit a post-dated check early;
- take or threaten to take your property unless it can be done legally; or
- contact you by postcard.

Can I control which debts my payments apply to?

Yes. If a debt collector is trying to collect more than one debt from you, the collector must apply any payment you make to the debt you select. Equally important, a debt collector may not apply a payment to a debt you don't think you owe.

Can a debt collector garnish my bank account or my wages?

If you don't pay a debt, a creditor or its debt collector generally can sue you to collect. If they win, the court will enter a judgment against you. The judgment states the amount of money you owe, and allows the creditor or collector to get a garnishment order against you, directing a third party, like your bank, to turn over funds from your account to pay the debt.

Wage garnishment happens when your employer withholds part of your compensation to pay your debts. Your wages usually can be garnished only as the result of a court order. Don't ignore a lawsuit summons. If you do, you lose the opportunity to fight a wage garnishment.

Can federal benefits be garnished?

Many federal benefits are exempt from garnishment, including:

- Social Security Benefits
- Supplemental Security Income (SSI) Benefits
- Veterans' Benefits
- Civil Service and Federal Retirement and Disability Benefits
- Service Members' Pay
- Military Annuities and Survivors' Benefits
- Student Assistance
- Railroad Retirement Benefits
- Merchant Seamen Wages
- Longshoremen's and Harbor Workers' Death and Disability Benefits
- Foreign Service Retirement and Disability Benefits
- Compensation for Injury, Death, or Detention of Employees of U.S. Contractors outside the U.S.
- Federal Emergency Management Agency Federal Disaster Assistance

But federal benefits may be garnished under certain circumstances, including to pay delinquent taxes, alimony, child support, or student loans.

Do I have any recourse if I think a debt collector has violated the law?

You have the right to sue a collector in a state or federal court within one year from the date the law was violated. If you win, the judge can require the collector to pay you for any damages you can prove you suffered because of the illegal collection practices, like lost wages and medical bills.

The judge can require the debt collector to pay you up to $1,000, even if you can't prove that you suffered actual damages. You also can be reimbursed for your attorney's fees and court costs. A group of people also may sue a debt collector as part of a class action lawsuit and recover money for damages up to $500,000, or one percent of the collector's net worth, whichever amount is lower. Even if a debt collector violates the FDCPA in trying to collect a debt, the debt does not go away if you owe it.

What should I do if a debt collector sues me?

If a debt collector files a lawsuit against you to collect a debt, respond to the lawsuit, either personally or through your lawyer, by the date specified in the court papers to preserve your rights.

Where do I report a debt collector for an alleged violation?

Report any problems you have with a debt collector to your state Attorney General's office (www.naag.org) and the Federal Trade Commission (www.ftc.gov). Many states have their own debt collection laws that are different from the federal Fair Debt Collection Practices Act. Your Attorney General's office can help you determine your rights under your state's law.

For More Information

To learn more about debt collection and other credit-related issues, visit www.ftc.gov/credit and MyMoney.gov, the U.S. government's portal to financial education.

The FTC works for the consumer to prevent fraudulent, deceptive, and unfair business practices in the marketplace and to provide information to help consumers spot, stop, and avoid them. To file a complaint or to get free information on consumer issues, visit ftc.gov or call toll-free, 1-877-FTC-HELP (1-877-382-4357); TTY: 1-866-653-4261. The FTC enters consumer complaints into the Consumer Sentinel Network, a secure online database and investigative tool used by hundreds of civil and criminal law enforcement agencies in the United States and abroad.

This page intentionally left blank

ABOUT THE AUTHORS

Dean Roush is Director of Finance for an outreach ministry. In past endeavors he was a bank Vice-President, an accounting manager for a multi-state graphics arts company, and a computer software developer and information technology consultant. He received his BS in Computer Science from West Texas A&M University.

Marsue Roush is an auditor and Certified Public Accountant. For many years she held various financial and managerial positions at a large electric utility and two of its subsidiaries. She received her BA in Accounting from West Texas A&M University.

More information is available at www.truplan.org.

This page intentionally left blank

www.ingramcontent.com/pod-product-compliance
Lightning Source LLC
Chambersburg PA
CBHW051328170526
45166CB00002B/726